HOW TO BE
PENTECOSTAL

With
Spea
To

Also by Tony Campolo

Partly Right
A Reasonable Faith
It's Friday, but Sunday's Coming'
You Can Make a Difference
Who Switched the Price Tags?
20 Hot Potatoes Christians Are Afraid to Touch
The Kingdom of God Is a Party

with Bart Campolo
Things We Wish We Had Said

TONY CAMPOLO

HOW TO BE

PENTECOSTAL

Without Speaking in Tongues

THOMAS NELSON PUBLISHERS
Nashville

How to Be Pentecostal Without Speaking in Tongues

Scripture quotations are from the King James Version.

Library of Congress Cataloging-in-Publication Data:

Campolo, Anthony.
    How to be Pentecostal without speaking in tongues / Anthony Campolo.
        p.   cm.
    ISBN 0–8499–0884–1
    ISBN 0–8499–3569–5 (tp)
    1. Holy Spirit.   2. Pentecostalism.   I. Title.
BT121.2.C25   1991
234'.13—dc20   91–17220
                                                       CIP

4 5 6 7 8 9 LBM 7 6 5 4 3 2 1

Printed in the United States of America

To my charismatic baby granddaughter

Miranda Sarah Campolo

Contents

Introduction

This is a book about the most important thing going on in the world—the work of the Holy Spirit.

It is almost impossible to go anywhere in Christendom these days without coming across some evidence of the growing Charismatic movement. In Latin America it is sweeping people into Pentecostal churches in phenomenal numbers. In England there is constant talk of the "signs and wonders" of the Kingdom of God that are being wrought under the power of the Spirit. Across the United States Pentecostal churches are growing in leaps and bounds even as mainline churches shift into rapid decline. This book is about these remarkable movements of the Spirit.

Some of what goes on under the name of the Charismatic movement has become known as the Renewal movement. Staid churches are experiencing new vitality as the Spirit blows away the cobwebs that gathered during their more lethargic days. Young people are being challenged to be missionaries and evangelists in record numbers. New forms of worship are waking people up to new joys on Sunday morning. Small groups are forming that are providing mutual love and support for persons who hitherto felt weak and alone.

But there is a downside to all of this. Like any good thing that comes from God there are abuses by those who want to use the things of God for selfish purposes. There are phonies who are gaining wealth and prestige by claiming to have special gifts from God. And there are practices that hide behind the guise of being initiated by the Holy Spirit, but they are nothing more than the cheap tricks of charlatans.

This book is an attempt to help the uninitiated to understand what is going on in this wonderful, mystical, exciting, dangerous, and confusing world of the emerging Charismatic movement. It is an attempt to clarify what is happening; to provide a handle on some of the terms and vocabulary used by charismatics; and to perceive what is real and what is phony. Most importantly, however, these pages should spell out for those who are not charismatics how the Spirit becomes a dynamic presence in the lives of those Christians who know that there is more to being a Christian than just believing the right doctrines and practicing the right rituals.

The Holy Spirit always upsets the status quo. The Spirit disrupts the old order of things and ushers in a new openness. The Spirit is the new wine in the old wineskins and the new cloth on the old garment. Those who want everything to remain as it was ought not to get involved with the things of the Spirit, because the ministry of the Spirit makes all things new: "Therefore if any man be in Christ, he is a new creature: old things are passed away; behold, all things are become new" (2 Cor. 5:17).

The Charismatic Movement

Chapter 1

Something's Blowin' in the Wind

Pentecostalism just isn't what it used to be, at least so far as outsiders are concerned. Those in the mainstream churches no longer view the Charismatic movement as laughable "holy-rollers" pumped into uncontrolled hysterics by semi-charlatans. Such images, if they were ever true, have been more than obliterated by members of their own congregations who have been changed in positive ways by the so-called infilling of the Spirit. There are just too many Presbyterians, Episcopalians, and Roman Catholics who talk of spiritual deliverance and physical healing for there to be a broad denial that something good and miraculous is taking place across the land and around the world. The evidence is obvious.

Several years ago I visited a small town in the Dominican Republic (let us call it El Sebo) in order to meet with a faithful fundamentalist minister who was serving there. The town was a mess in every sense. Trash was everywhere. Garbage clogged the open sewers. Bodies of stripped cars cluttered every vacant lot, and the houses of the town seemed tumbled down, dirty, and neglected. It was one of those poor towns that elicits pity for those who are destined to make it their home.

The missionary whom I visited talked about how little progress he had seen during more than a decade of ministry. There were less than a dozen people who belonged to his little church. And this handful of Christians worked very hard to keep from falling back into the cesspool of degradation that seemed evident everywhere around them. The bars and cantinas of the town did a hefty business, and drunkenness was common. Perhaps the only thing that might have been more common than drunkenness was sexual promiscuity. The young men of the town were anxious to prove their machismo and worked overtime trying to hustle every available female into bed. The old men talked with a strange kind of reluctant pride of the many children around town that they had fathered out of wedlock. The official religion of the town was Roman Catholic, but the real religion was a combination of some folk myths and superstitions mixed with voodoo.

To say the least, El Sebo was depressing. The missionary was discouraged. He seemed to be doing little more than going though the motions of evangelizing and teaching. And he had seemingly little expectation that anything good would come from his efforts.

"God will judge us for our faithfulness, not for our success," he reminded me. That being true, this dear saint of God was sure to be judged faithful on that final day when we all stand before the Eternal Throne, for being faithful was about all he was.

"What this town needs is a revival!" he declared to me. "Only God Himself coming down and performing a miracle can change things around here."

And I readily agreed.

A little over four years later I had an occasion to revisit El Sebo. And when I arrived in town I was overtaken immediately with the obvious evidence of change. "Maybe the sun is shining brighter today," I said to myself. "Maybe I remember things as being worse than they really were. Perhaps these seemingly happy people greeting each other with friendly smiles were really not as beaten down as my memory pictured them. Maybe my perception of things was mistaken."

The streets were relatively free of trash and debris. I didn't see any drunks around. The houses seemed to have a bright, scrubbed look about them. To tell the truth, El Sebo did not seem to be all that bad a place to live and raise a family.

When I caught up with my missionary friend he assured me it was not my imagination. He explained that it was not only the way the town looked that was different, the people themselves were changed.

"The drinking has dropped off," he reported. "The young people are not doing many of the immoral things they used to do, so there aren't many teenage girls becoming pregnant. I'll even have to admit that many people are married now who just used to live together before."

The economy of El Sebo had changed too. The onetime feeble coffee business was prospering because the workers had eliminated their middle man. They had gotten together and chipped in to buy their own truck and were delivering their coffee to the market themselves. Their increased income apparently had stimulated the development of better coffee plants, and the creation of a co-op had enabled them to challenge the exploitive practices of the old general store. Their growing coffee industry had spun off at least ten to fifteen cottage industries, which in turn had created jobs for scores of the townspeople. El Sebo might be something less than it should be, but it was certainly a far cry from what it used to be.

My missionary friend explained the cause for all of these changes. "It's the priest," he said, with a bit of anger in his voice. "That priest went down to Santo Domingo and got wrapped up with some Charismatics. When he got back here, he worked overtime spreading all of that false doctrine, and the people bought what he told them. His church is packed now, not only for Sunday masses, but two or three times during the week for those praise services he holds. He's made half of this town into Charismatics, and El Sebo just isn't the same anymore."

"You don't seem to be pleased by all of this," I responded.

"Why should I be?" was his retort. "All of these seemingly good things that you see happening are only Satan's way of confusing people and getting more of them into that deceptive Pentecostalism."

He went on to explain how he believed that all that was going on under the leadership of that charismatic priest was nothing more than a cover-up for the "sneaky work of the Evil One." It was his opinion that Satan knew that "real" revival was about to break out in that town and had started this Charismatic movement to keep it from happening.

I couldn't believe my ears. Did he really believe that Satan had done all of this good just to keep the people of that town from getting converted to his Dispensationalist theology? Could he see all the changes that were taking place around him and honestly not attribute them to God? Of course the answer to these questions is *yes!*

When Jesus was confronted by those who saw his good works and then attributed them to Satan, He declared,

> . . . Every kingdom divided against itself is brought to desolation; and every city or house divided against itself shall not stand: and if Satan cast out Satan, he is divided against himself; how shall then his kingdom stand? And if I by Beelzebub cast out devils, by whom do your children cast them out? therefore they shall be your judges. But if I cast out devils by the Spirit of God, then the Kingdom of God is come unto you.
>
> *Matthew 12:25–28*

I was so startled by my friend's judgment that I failed to give him the warning that Jesus gave to those who could look at the works of the Holy Spirit and not recognize them:

10

Either make the tree good, and his fruit good; or else make the tree corrupt, and his fruit corrupt: for the tree is known by his fruit. O generation of vipers, how can ye, being evil, speak good things? for out of the abundance of the heart the mouth speaketh.

Matthew 12:33

Across Latin America the Charismatic movement is bringing millions into a changed and holy lifestyle. In Australia, New Zealand, and the United Kingdom the flames of a charismatic revival are beginning to burn. There are healings and miracles reported everywhere. Pentecostal churches have become the fastest growing churches in America. We cannot deny what the facts reveal. The Charismatic movement has become the most dynamic expression of Christianity in the world today.

On the other hand, I am not denying that there have been abuses and that some strange things have gone on in the name of Pentecostalism. The scriptures do commend us to be discerning about what is going on in the name of the Holy Spirit: "Beloved, believe not every spirit, but try the spirits whether they are of God: because many false prophets are gone out into the world" (1 John 4:1). It is a Christian responsibility to examine what is going on in all facets of this growing religious phenomenon. This is particularly important at a time when there is so much phoniness and deception in Pentecostalism.

As a case in point, there was a well-known West Coast preacher who claimed to possess all kinds of charismatic powers. During revivals and crusades he exercised one of these powers by being able to pick out people in the audience who had some very specific problems or physical ailments. He then could proceed to "prophesy" solutions to those problems and pronounce healings for those whom he picked out as having specific sicknesses and infirmities. With his face strained and his eyes closed he would say something like: "There is someone here tonight whose sister in Fresno, California is suffering with cancer. God wants to heal

11

your sister so that she can go on raising her three young daughters and her new baby boy. You know who you are. Would you please stand so that we can lay hands on you and pray for her recovery?"

Then some befuddled man would stand and, with tears streaming down his cheeks, cry out, "It's me! Oh, Reverend, please pray for my sister and please pray for me!"

The detailed specifics about the sick woman would leave little doubt in anyone's mind that this charismatic evangelist had a special gift of discernment from God. There would be "Ohs" and "Ahs" of amazement throughout the crowd. As he worked his magic the miraculous appeared to be happening right before their eyes. People could not help but be impressed.

The fame and fortune of this particular evangelist grew nightly. The offering plates were constantly filled. The crowds regularly grew in numbers. He was, as they say, "on a roll."

Then came the exposé. One cynical member of the congregation noticed that the evangelist had a hearing aid. He wondered why a man with such a great gift of healing could not take care of his own particular problem.

His suspicions were confirmed when he brought a high-frequency radio receiver to a subsequent meeting and was able to intercept messages that the evangelist's wife was sending him from a back room. What was really happening was that prior to the start of the meeting, the evangelist's wife mingled with the crowd and picked up specific information about various people in the audience. She would ask questions and overhear conversations. Later, when the evangelist was in the midst of his performance, she would radio this information to him. As he walked up and down the aisles of the auditorium preaching and "healing," she would feed him the facts he needed to look like someone with a direct line to God.

What made matters worse was that this particular evangelist was exposed on Johnny Carson's "Tonight Show." The man who had figured out what was going on had made recordings of the radio conversations he intercepted between the evangelist and his wife, and he played them for the entertainment of millions of American television viewers. Carson mockingly remarked how God's voice and the voice of the evangelist's wife were almost identical. The audience laughed, but many of us who believe in a God who can perform miracles were in pain. It is always painful to those of the church when one of their members is publicly disgraced. "Whether one member suffer, all the members suffer with it" (1 Cor. 12:26).

Not all phoniness in the Charismatic movement is quite so blatant and purposefully deceptive. Let me give you an example of how a well-meaning person can hurt the integrity of legitimate Pentecostalism.

It has been almost a decade since I was the speaker for an unusual graduation service in Washington, D.C. Some men had come to know Christ as personal Savior and Lord while in prison, and they had completed a training course to equip them to be more effective witnesses while continuing to serve their time behind bars. I had spent some time with these men the afternoon preceding the evening graduation. I had heard their painful stories and was a bit broken by the tragedies they related to me.

One man had raped a seventeen-year-old girl who had lived down the street from him. He was a Christian now, but his wife and children, nevertheless, had refused to forgive him and never wanted to see him again.

Another man was guilty of armed robbery. His elderly mother was now dying of cancer and was crying to see him before she died, but he could not go to her.

Another had severely beaten his wife and children, but in spite of his professed conversion they had rejected him and had taken someone else to be the husband and father for the family.

The stories went on and on, heartbreak after heartbreak, tragedy after tragedy.

During the graduation exercises and just before I was to speak, a woman rose to sing. She was the special music for the program. But before she sang she said, "There are just a few words I'd like to share with you before I sing." I wish she hadn't.

"On the way over here tonight," she said, "I was driving my new station wagon. It's less than two weeks old. I was driving right behind a big truck carrying a load of stones. One of the stones fell off the truck, hit the highway, bounced up, and hit my windshield. It put a nick in the glass. I was so depressed.

"When I got out of the car to come in here, I put my finger on that nick and prayed a simple prayer that God would heal it. And would you believe that when I removed my finger that nick was gone?"

"No," mumbled several of the men in an all too audible manner.

The woman, embarrassed that her healing-of-the-windshield story had not gone over better, cleared her throat and proceeded to sing.

These are only two examples, but these sorts of abuses and trivializations of the work of the Holy Spirit have given the Charismatic movement a bad name. We must not, however, allow some phonies and some sincere but misguided persons to turn us off to what may be an era of unusual outpourings of the Holy Spirit. We must not let abuses blind us to some of the greatest blessings the world has seen since Pentecost.

Chapter 2

How Did Something So Strange Get So Popular?

To understand what is going on in the various Pentecostal movements of our time we need a little background to get ourselves oriented. Pentecostalism, which is the focus of our attention in this section, had its modern beginnings in the now somewhat famous 1906 Azuza Street prayer meeting in Los Angeles. A group of Christian leaders had come together to pray for a special outpouring of the Holy Spirit and for the beginning of a spiritual revival in America.

Before that particular meeting was over, many people were praying and worshiping God in "tongues." A powerful presence was felt, and something new was ushered into American Christianity. Out of this humble start the Assembly of God churches had their beginning and the modern Pentecostal movement got underway.

Opposition to Pentecostalism was almost immediate from the struggling Fundamentalist movement. Trying to fend off the rationalism of theological liberalism that had people questioning the validity and the authority of scriptures, the Fundamentalists, all of a sudden, were fighting a war on a second front—against emerging charismatic Christianity.

To the Fundamentalists, Pentecostals appeared dangerous, not because they questioned the authority of scripture, but because they seemed to have a second source of authority that was far too subjective for their liking. Pentecostals, as the Fundamentalists perceived them, claimed some kind of a special hot line to God and always came up with some kind of "word from the Lord." It was this claim of direct revelation to individuals made by the Holy Spirit that made the Pentecostals more than suspect. Fundamentalists had become the heirs of Luther's famous dictum, *sola scriptura*, and they were not about to be swept away by what seemed to them to be an alternative source of revelation.

Abuses of the claim to special revelations do occur. They usually are in the "independent" charismatic churches. In Pentecostal denominations, such as the Assembly of God, there are institutionalized means for preventing behavior that deviates from biblical norms.

I know of a minister of an independent charismatic church in Nevada who claimed to have had a word from the Lord telling him to divorce his wife and marry another woman. This could never have happened in an Assembly of God church or in any of the other "recognized" Pentecostal denominations.

Some Fundamentalists, particularly those in the Reformed tradition, and Dispensationalists (those who subscribe to the theology of John Darby and follow the teachings outlined in the Scofield Reference Bible) have another reason for rejecting Pentecostal claims. They believe that the gifts of the Spirit outlined in 1 Corinthians 12:7–11 were meant only for the early church and not for the church of today:

> But the manifestation of the Spirit is given to every man to profit withal. For to one is given by the Spirit the word of wisdom; to another the word of knowledge by the same Spirit; to another faith by the same Spirit; to another the gifts of healing by the same Spirit; to another the working of miracles; to

another prophecy; to another discerning of spirits; to another divers kinds of tongues; to another the interpretation of tongues: but all these worketh that one and the selfsame Spirit, dividing to every man severally as he will.

According to their beliefs, these special gifts were necessary for early Christians to have a basis for authority and direction in ministry until they had the completed New Testament. When the canon of the Bible was completed, they say, then gifts such as the gifts of knowledge, tongues, and prophesy became superfluous and "passed away." In their reading of the well-known thirteenth chapter of 1 Corinthians they claim that when the Apostle Paul refers to "that which is perfect," he is referring to the completed New Testament:

> Charity never faileth: but whether there be prophecies, they shall fail; whether there be tongues, they shall cease; whether there be knowledge, it shall vanish away. For we know in part, and we prophesy in part. But when *that which is perfect* is come, then that which is in part shall be done away.
>
> vv. 8–10 *(emphasis mine)*

Consequently, they believe that the gifts of the Spirit are no longer operative and that any exercising of these gifts is at best the misguided work of someone's imagination, at worst the work of the devil. Such a doctrinal position poses a great barrier to mutual acceptance between Charismatics and traditional Fundamentalists.

Things are changing, however. The spectacular success of the Charismatic movement, both in other countries and here in the United States, has led many, if not most, Fundamentalists to give some consideration to changing their views.

In Latin America the amazing growth of charismatic churches is such that two countries—Honduras and Brazil—will most likely be predominantly Protestant by the end of the twentieth century.

Already in Brazil more Protestants attend church on Sunday than do Catholics, and the overwhelming proportion of them are new "born-again" charismatics.

In England there are rudimentary signs of revival in a nation that many social commentators previously had claimed had moved into a post-Christian era. Starting with the Billy Graham Evangelistic Crusade of the early 1950s, house churches have revitalized parish churches, and a host of parachurch organizations, such as Youth for Christ, have led the way for a Renewal movement in British Christianity.

All of these dynamic expressions of Christianity have, over the last two decades, come to participate in the Charismatic movement. From Rob White, the executive director of British Youth for Christ, to Clive Calver, the head of the Evangelical Alliance, the leadership in the contemporary English Renewal movement has come to be strongly supportive of the Charismatic movement. The same is true of the leadership that is nurturing the revival movements in New Zealand and Australia.

Youth with a Mission, which has more than thirty-two thousand young people serving as missionaries around the world, is now the largest missionary organization in the world. Its leader, Loren Cunningham, is very much a part of this charismatic revival. His visions and prophetic messages in the Spirit have given a direction and a theology to this movement that many claim has become one of the most vital expressions of evangelism in our time.

Personally, I believe that Christian television broadcasting, more than anything else, has gained acceptance for Pentecostalism both from Fundamentalists as well as from mainline denominations. Even in spite of the falls of Jimmy Swaggart and Jim Bakker, two of the more popular Pentecostal televangelists, charismatic Christianity has continued to have a wide television viewing audience.

Pat Robertson, a charismatic Baptist, has provided one of the most significant contributions toward this end. His program, viewed by millions daily, and his serious run for the presidency of the United States in 1988 have gained recognition and support for him and his brand of charismatic Christianity from people throughout the country. Pastors of local churches dare not put down Robertson's television show, "The 700 Club," without the likelihood of offending some of their members who are favorably disposed to it.

Among the guests on "The 700 Club" have been people such as Billy Graham and Francis Schaeffer, two of the most respected voices of the evangelical community. Political figures ranging from Pat Buchanan to Mark Hatfield have also appeared on his show. And Robertson does not confine his invitations to those on the religious and political right. Ron Sider and others on the evangelical left also have had their chances to be heard on his program.

Robertson's television show features conservative political commentary, and he has gained a popularity with those of the New Right who are part of the respected Republican establishment. His rational style and calm presentations have made him an acceptable voice in Middle America.

In the midst of all of his social and political views, Robertson also articulates a message of charismatic Christianity that places a strong emphasis on the healing ministry of the Holy Spirit. Thus, Pentecostalism, through Robertson, has gained considerable respectability.

The worship styles of the Charismatic movement also have contributed to the growing acceptance of Pentecostalism throughout Christendom. The introduction of worship songs that include "Majesty" and "Shine, Jesus, Shine" have given church services a new genre of music. It has been the Charismatic movement that has made guitars and electric pianos so familiar at Sunday worship that they are threatening to replace organs.

Acceptance is a two-way street. Not only has mainstream and fundamentalist religion gradually become more accepting of Pentecostalism, but Pentecostalism in return has become more accepting of Fundamentalism. Up until relatively recent days it was common for those who had experienced a charismatic infilling of the Holy Spirit to regard other Christians as being in a kind of second-class category, if they regarded them as being Christians at all. It was common among Pentecostals to associate the charismatic experience with being "saved" so that those who had not had this experience were viewed as devoid of the regenerating power of God. Furthermore, those Pentecostals who held to this narrow view usually believed that anyone filled with the Spirit could be expected to pray and worship in tongues. Needless to say, such beliefs estab-lished an insurmountable barrier between Pentecostals and those to whom tongues seemed foreign and strange.

All of this has changed over the last decade. Attitudes changed as non-Pentecostals appeared on the television shows of charismatic televangelists and as they came to be speakers at various Pentecostal gatherings. Pentecostals gradually learned to resonate to what they were hearing from people who made no claim to ever having prayed in tongues. Consequently they increasingly felt a spiritual kinship to those who were outside the charismatic fold. This did not water down the importance of the charismatic experience in the minds of Pentecostals. It simply put it in a new perspective. That new perspective was made very clear to me by a Pentecostal pastor who said, "Praying in tongues does not make me a better Christian than you, but it does make me a better Christian than I would have been had I not acquired this gift."

Most Pentecostals have this perspective, even if they don't put it so clearly. Attitudes of spiritual superiority are becoming minimal among those who are accepting this new way of regarding noncharismatics.

The Longing for Something More

The most important basis for the growing acceptance of Pentecostal Christianity is a basic hunger in the human psyche for a taste of the miraculous. The truth is that most Christians have a basic dissatisfaction with the quality of their spiritual life and long for something more and something deeper. There is within most of us an insatiable appetite for the supernatural, and mundane Christianity leaves us wanting. We all long for the assurances of God's reality in our lives. Rational theologies do not seem to satisfy us, and we look for the ecstasies that are described by the mystics.

Which of us has not wished that we had been with Jesus and had seen Him feeding the five thousand? Which of us has not wondered what it would have been like to see Him heal the man who had been blind since birth? And how many of us think that we would never have a spiritual doubt again if we could just see a bona fide miracle? Are we not all a bit like Thomas? Don't we want a resurrected Jesus whom we can see and touch?

The Charismatic movement has spokespersons who know how to capitalize on such spiritual hungers. John Wimber is one of them. As the founder of one of the newest Pentecostal denominations, he claims that most of us have such encounters with the miraculous and are spoken to directly by God daily. The problem, says Wimber, is that we do not have the eyes to see or the ears to hear what the Spirit is trying to communicate to us. He argues that the cause of this indifference to the miraculous as it constantly impinges on our lives is that we have been socialized into a world-view that conditions us to discount such things when they occur. When God tries to communicate with us through "signs and wonders," we tend to explain away such revelations by looking for some "scientific" or rational explanation so that we can fit them in with what society has told us is real. Undoubtedly there is some truth to this.

When I was doing my graduate studies I had the privilege of working under Paul Van Buren, a scholar who gained notoriety as one of the God-Is-Dead theologians. Steeped in the philosophy of logical positivism, Van Buren accepted no theological statement that could not be verified by empirical means. Needless to say we had many confrontations concerning what is "true" about the gospel. Our times together were seldom peaceful.

In one of our discussions, Dr. Van Buren tried to explain to me that it just was not possible in the modern world to talk about God in the same way that people did in prescientific Bible days.

"Quite simply," he said to me, "you can't do what Elijah did to prove that your God is real. You are not about to prove the existence of God by building an altar of wood, dousing it with water, and then inviting the campus skeptics to watch as you pray down fire from heaven. Things like that don't happen in our kind of world, and even religious people no longer expect that kind of miracle."

"But," I responded, "suppose I did all of those things. Suppose I built the altar. Suppose I doused it with water. And suppose I prayed down fire from heaven, and fire *did* come down and *did* consume the altar . . . what would you say?"

Van Buren paused a moment, and then with a sly smile in one corner of his mouth he replied, "I'd say that there has to be another explanation."

This is what Wimber is talking about when he says that we are conditioned to interpret reality in the context of what sociologists and philosophers call a modern *Weltanschauung*, or world-view. We tend to explain away the miraculous even when it hits us in the face. In a scientific world we are conditioned to make miracles fit in our "rational" scheme of things.

A Touch of the Miraculous

There was an event in my life that definitely had the marks of the miraculous. It was one of those moments that is hard to put

24

into either category of reason or science, even though in times of doubt I am tempted to try. It was a miracle that is difficult to explain away. Yet those are times when I discount or even wonder whether I imagined the whole thing.

When I was fourteen years old, my family was very poor, and my father was out of work because he had been struck down with Hodgkin's disease. His hospitalization insurance was running out, and we did not know where we would get enough money to meet our basic needs. I knew that it was my duty to earn some money for my family, but at the same time I wanted to stay in school, get good grades, and go on to college.

I figured out that I could buy unsold loaves of bread that truck drivers returned to the Bond Bread Company located at Fifty-sixth and Market Streets. I could buy the bread for a nickel a loaf and sell it for a quarter a loaf to restaurants throughout West Philadelphia. The transaction promised a hefty profit, but there were a couple of problems. I could not pick up the bread until after 9:00 P.M., and the only means I had for delivering the bread was by piling it on a wagon that I pulled behind my bike.

Surprisingly, things worked out. I began to make enough money to help out at home, and I was still able to keep up with my schoolwork.

One dark, cold, rainy night at about a quarter to eleven I was making a delivery. Unfortunately I rode my bike over a pothole. Suddenly there was a *bang!* My front tire blew out. I pulled the bike off the street and sat down on the curb. After a while I started to cry. I remember crying hard and long. I was soaked, shivering, and completely discouraged. It was a lonely side street. There was no one to hear me when I cried out loud, "God, you're mean. Everybody else thinks you're kind. But I know you're mean. If you were kind you'd help me."

I cried for a few minutes more, then, for reasons that I will never figure out, I got up and pushed my bike and my load of bread to the service station down the street. The station was closed for the night. Nevertheless, I pushed my bike over to the air pump and tried to put air into the blown-out tire.

It never occurred to me how unusual it was that the air pump of this closed service station was still working. I was in such a state of brokenness and sadness that I did what I did in a daze. Needless to say the air came out of the tear in the blown-out tire as quickly as I pumped it in. I don't know what I was expecting. But trembling and crying I just stayed there in the dark carrying out a hopeless task.

Then the miracle happened! Suddenly I realized that the tire was hard. Somehow and in some way that is impossible to explain, the tire was holding air. I stood up, confused but happy. I remember yelling out loud, "Oh, thank you! Oh, thank you!"

I made two more deliveries and then rode the bike three miles back to my house. And the tire held!

When I got home I lifted the bike onto my front porch and locked it. The time was just after 12:30 A.M. I went to the front door and was putting my key into the lock when I heard a hissing sound. I turned back to the bike and watched with amazement as the air quickly left the blown-out tire. The miracle was over, and the tire went flat.

God had gotten me home. He had not let me suffer beyond that which I was able to bear. He performed a miracle for me because only a miracle could have saved my faith on that painful evening. God knew that somehow, if something had not happened, I would have given up—not just on life, but on Him as well.

> There hath no temptation taken you but such as is common to man: but God is faithful, who will not suffer you to be tempted above that ye are able; but will with the temptation also make a way to escape, that ye may be able to bear it.
> *1 Corinthians 10:13*

You would think that after such an experience I would never have any spiritual doubts again. But I do. And at such times I think that there must be some "natural" explanation for what happened to that tire that dismal night.

Wimber is right. In the modern scientific world in which we live, we are tempted to explain away everything that does not fit into the logical categories that go with the societally approved, rational mind-set.

But the craving for the miraculous still goes on. We still look for signs and wonders to affirm what we want to believe about God. We still long for the ecstasies that will transport us into that state of spirituality where there are no doubts, only inner peace.

In such a world and in such a state of consciousness we welcome Pentecostals. They talk of miracles that they have seen and heard. To them the supernatural is a common occurrence that elicits little more than a quiet "Thank you, Jesus!" They give testimonies to having total satisfaction in their hearts and of being possessed with an absolute confidence of their salvation.

Such talk gives all of us pause, because that is what we all want—yea—it is what we all crave. That is why non-Pentecostals cannot walk away from those who talk of having had a charismatic experience and say, "Who needs it?" Because, down deep inside, all of us know we do.

Chapter 3

Talking the Same Language

efore we go any further, I think it best that we define some terms and explain what Pentecostals are talking about when they refer to such things as "speaking in tongues," "having the gift of prophesy," and "having a word from the Lord." There is no doubt that Pentecostals seem to have developed a system of religious hieroglyphics that leave those outside their fold somewhat confused and more than a bit intimidated. Some clarifications about Pentecostal terminology are essential if the rest of us are to know what they are talking about.

First of all, when Pentecostals talk of speaking in tongues they usually aren't referring to speaking in tongues at all. They usually are referring to *praying* in tongues. Speaking in tongues is useless unless there is someone around who has the gift of interpretation (1 Cor. 14:27). Such is not the case for praying in tongues. This latter gift is simply a way of expressing love and yearnings for God that are too deep to be put into the common language of the culture.

Speaking in tongues occurs when an individual becomes a "mouthpiece for God" and has a special message from God for the church. The "words" that such a person utters are in an "unknown language." The apostle Paul contends that when someone is exercising this gift, someone should be on hand who has the gift of interpretation (1 Cor. 12:10). Otherwise, says Paul, all that we have on our hands are some vain babblings:

> If any man speak in an unknown tongue, let it be by two, or at the most by three, and that by course; and let one interpret. But if there be no interpreter, let him keep silence in the church; and let him speak to himself, and to God. . . . For God is not the author of confusion, but of peace, as in all churches of the saints.
>
> *1 Corinthians 14:27–28, 33*

Praying in tongues is quite another thing. Sometimes the feelings and yearnings of a Christian are so intense and so profound that the ordinary words of human languages cannot express them. There are occasions when what is happening in the mind is so awesome that there are no words in the common vocabulary that can convey its meaning. According to Pentecostals, it is in such times that the individual can become surrendered to God and let the Holy Spirit prompt in him or her prayers and praise in sounds that make no sense to anyone who may be listening. These sounds are not meant to be interpreted because they are *not* a message from God. Instead these "words" are "groanings" of the heart of the Christian. They are feelings toward God and they are sounds which only God understands and appreciates.

Paul writes:

> Likewise the Spirit also helpeth our infirmities: for we know not what we should pray for as we ought: but the Spirit itself maketh intercession for us with groanings which cannot be uttered. And he that searcheth the hearts knoweth what is the mind of the Spirit, because he maketh intercession for the saints according to the will of God.
>
> *Romans 8:26–27*

When Christians pray in tongues they claim that the Holy Spirit prays *through* them. In other words, praying in tongues is the Holy Spirit flowing through the Christian and giving praise to the Father, carrying the Christian's unarticulated needs to the Father. Praying in tongues is when the Christian allows something from the depths within to flow out toward God. It is not meant for understanding and is not meant to add knowledge to the church. Again Paul writes: "For if I pray in an unknown tongue, my spirit prayeth, but my understanding is unfruitful" (1 Cor. 14:14).

The Gifts and the Fruit

The next thing to clarify is the difference between the *gifts* of the Spirit and the *fruit* of the Spirit. When the Bible speaks of the gifts of the Spirit it is referring to special talents and abilities that God gives to Christians so that they can provide for the church all the services that are needed for it to carry out its mission. The church needs preachers, so, according to the scriptures, God gives to the church persons who have the gift of preaching (i.e., the gift of prophesy). The church needs teachers to provide clarity concerning the essential doctrines of the faith, so God provides special people to meet that need. The church needs missionaries (i.e., apostles) and evangelists to win converts, and the Bible teaches that we can count on God to raise up people who have the gifts to fulfill these roles. Concerning the *gifts* of the Spirit the Book of Ephesians says:

> And he gave some, apostles; and some, prophets; and some, evangelists; and some, pastors and teachers; For the perfecting of the saints, for the work of the ministry, for the edifying of the body of Christ: till we all come in the unity of the faith, and of the knowledge of the Son of God, unto a perfect man, unto the measure of the stature of the fulness of Christ.
> *Ephesians 4:11–13*

Not all of these gifts are spectacular in nature. Actually, the Apostle Paul makes a strong point out of the fact that those who have the "up-front" gifts that get them public recognition may not be the most important to the life and maintenance of the church:

Nay, much more those members of the body, which seem to be more feeble, are necessary: And those members of the body, which we think to be less honourable, upon these we bestow more abundant honour; and our uncomely parts have more abundant comeliness.

1 Corinthians 12:22–23

This became very apparent to me one day when I went to speak at a small country church in Indiana.

I arrived at the church about an hour before the service, went in and took a seat in the front pew. After a few minutes an elderly man came into the sanctuary and went about checking to see that everything was in order. He made sure that the thermostat was set at the right temperature and that the windows were opened just the right amount to allow for proper ventilation. He went up and down every pew to see if there was a hymn book and a Bible in every place.

When he got to where I was seated I introduced myself as the preacher of the day. Then I asked him if he was the custodian of the church. No sooner had the words come out of my mouth than I knew I had made a mistake in asking.

"No!" he answered, in a somewhat gruff manner. "No, I'm not the custodian or anything like that! I'm just exercising a special gift of the Spirit."

I was intrigued and could not help but ask him exactly which of the gifts of the Spirit he believed that God had given him.

"The gift of helps," he answered. "Check it out in 1 Corinthians 12:28. You'll find it there. Paul talks about the gift of helps."

Indeed, he was right. Paul does mention that gift. Along with the more prominent gifts of healing, speaking in tongues, prophesying, and having words of knowledge, Paul mentions the gift of helps:

> And God hath set some in the church, first apostles, secondarily prophets, thirdly teachers, after that miracles, then gifts of healings, helps, governments, diversities of tongues.
>
> *1 Corinthians 12:28*

The old man went on to add, "You know we get a whole parade of preachers coming through here on their way to bigger and better things. Each of them stays for a few years and then moves on. Each of them thinks he's the best thing that this church has ever seen, and each of them thinks he's going to put this church on the map. Well after they're gone for a few years we have a hard time even remembering their names."

Then, pointing to himself he said proudly and with a big grin, "One of these days ole Harry's goin' to die, and the people of this church won't know what hit them. They'll come to church the next Sunday and find that nobody turned up the heat. They'll find out the hard way who shovelled the snow on all those winter days. And they'll take forever to figure out where half the stuff they need to run this church is stored away."

I'll bet he's right. This old saint, who had no official title and whose name wasn't listed in the church bulletin, undoubtedly had the gift of helps. And it's really hard to find somebody who is willing to exercise that gift for the body of Christ.

Indeed, there are, as the scriptures say, "diversities of gifts" in the body of Christ. But the Bible also refers to the *fruit* of the Spirit, which are qualities of personality that become evident in the lives of those who become "sanctified" Christians. The fruit of the Spirit are traits that become evident in those who yield themselves to the kind of transformation that God wants to bring about in His people. When, after making a commitment to Christ, a person becomes discipled into a godly lifestyle and seeks to grow into the likeness of Christ, certain changes begin to take place. Regular prayer, Bible study, and meditation on a personal level, coupled with serving the poor and standing up for the oppressed on the societal level, effect a metamorphosis for the Christian. According to Galatians 5, the following qualities become increasingly evident in the person's life:

> But the fruit of the Spirit is love, joy, peace, longsuffering, gentleness, goodness, faith, meekness, temperance: against such there is no law.
>
> *Galatians 5:22–23*

The Apostle Paul makes it clear that having the *fruit* of the Spirit is much more important than having the *gifts* of the Spirit. That is a major theme of the famous thirteenth chapter of 1 Corinthians. There Paul tells us that love, the primary fruit of the Spirit, is more important than any of the gifts. From this passage it is evident that love is the ultimate gift from God and the most important trait in a Christian's life.

> Though I speak with the tongues of men and of angels, and have not [love], I am become as sounding brass, or a tinkling cymbal. And though I have the gift of prophecy, and understand all mysteries, and all knowledge; and though I have all faith, so that I could remove mountains, and have not [love], I am nothing.
>
> *1 Corinthians 13:1–2*

It should be noted that sometimes those with the gifts of the Spirit are painfully lacking in the fruit of the Spirit. The fact that someone can preach up a storm or perform healings on the sick is no indication of that person's spiritual condition. Unfortunately, the gifts and the fruit do not necessarily go together.

One of the most painful realizations of my seminary days was that some of those who were the most gifted preachers gave little evidence of possessing the fruit of the Spirit. These men usually went on to become big-name leaders of large churches. On the other hand, there were those whose personal holiness was a thing of beauty, but lacking the gift of preaching they were consigned to churches in the sticks where no one would hear much from them again. For reasons that I find hard to understand, God often gives gifts to people who show few signs of being "spiritual" and just as often leaves those who very much "walk in the Spirit" with very few of the abilities needed to be outstanding leaders of His church.

J. Edwin Orr, the Irish revivalist, told of an evangelist he knew who was a very gifted preacher. This particular evangelist became sexually involved in an adulterous affair with the piano player on his crusade team. One night another member of the team, the song leader, accidentally walked into a bedroom in which he found the evangelist and this woman in an extremely compromising situation. The shocked song leader shouted at them and told them how disgusted he was. There was just one last night to the evangelistic crusade that they were conducting, so the song leader said he would lead the singing just one last time, but then he would be finished with the team forever.

The next night the corrupt evangelist preached brilliantly. The lusts of the flesh which had taken control of him seemed to provide little, if any, hindrance to his effectiveness. On the contrary, that night the evangelist seemed more effective than ever before.

When the invitation was given for people to come down the aisle and to give their lives to Christ, the response was overwhelming. Hundreds responded to the altar call. As the choir was singing the invitation hymn and the people were streaming forward, the evangelist leaned toward the song leader and arrogantly chided him by asking, "Well, how am I doing?"

There is no question about that evil man having the gift of evangelism. There is no doubt that people converted that night had a genuine experience with God. Yet the evangelist was lacking spirituality and was steeped in the lusts of the flesh.

All of this goes to show that God can draw straight lines with crooked sticks. He will use whom He will use. God is sovereign, and we have to learn that we cannot control who He chooses to manifest His power through and how He will do it.

Having some of the gifts of the Spirit may give those who possess them fame and recognition. But having the fruit of the Spirit is its own reward.

Having Words of Knowledge and Prophecy

There are other gifts of the Spirit that warrant our attention. We have to give some careful consideration to those who claim to have "a word from the Lord" and are exercising what they claim is the gift of the word of knowledge (1 Cor. 12:8). These are people who claim to receive special messages from God that they in turn are supposed to deliver to the church or to particular individuals as God instructs them.

I have people come up to me regularly with such messages just before or after I preach. Personally, I must admit that I am usually put off by most of these "gifted" people and discount what they tell me. However, I have to learn to be careful. After all, I may be cutting myself off from a revelation that I may very much need.

On one occasion after delivering a strong sermon in support of the Christian Feminist movement, a woman came up to me and handed me a book by Marabel Morgan. The book set forth some ideas that were out of sync with my own views.

The woman told me, "God spoke to me while you were speaking and told me to give you this book. He said to direct you to read it." She went on to explain that I should do as she instructed, because she had the gift of the word of knowledge and that what she had said was "a word from the Lord."

I thought that her gift and her message were a bit odd since I already had two copies of the book and had previously read through it a couple of times.

I do not doubt that there are people with "a word from the Lord," but it seems like a good many more people claim to have this gift of the word of knowledge than really do.

Another gift that is prominent in Pentecostal Christianity is the gift of prophecy. In the Bible the gift of prophecy does not necessarily involve making predictions about the future. In reality, to exercise the gift of prophecy is to *forthtell* the word of God. In more familiar terms, to prophesy is to preach the truths and judgments of God for this generation. With this *forth*telling there may be some *fore*telling, but that is only a secondary dimension of what is declared. The preacher may predict what will happen to the people if they do not heed the word of God and change their ways. But primary to prophecy is a declaration of what God expects His people to do and how He expects them to change.

All of this is a far cry from the kind of prophecy preaching that often comes across like a religious version of Jeanne Dixon. These so-called prophets who claim to be able to read the signs of the times and predict everything from when the Second Coming of Christ will take place to exactly who will be the anti-Christ do not belong in the same league with the real prophets of God.

I suppose my biggest complaint about these preachers who have so much to say about the end of the world is that they seldom pick up the theme that was primary in the prophetic utterances of the Bible. Unlike Jeremiah, Amos, Isaiah, and Jesus, they rarely if ever have a word of judgment against the exploitation of the poor or a condemnation of those who oppress the weak. Whereas the prophets of the Bible spoke for biblical justice, this new breed of "prophetic" entertainers make their living off giving the curious a peek into the future.

In some Pentecostal churches there is an important variant of the concept of prophecy that I have been describing. It is a form of prophecy in which the prophet is inspired by the Holy Spirit and then utters a message from God in the language of the congregation. In a charismatic Baptist church in Chula Vista, California, I had just finished a strong message against militarism. It had been a particularly difficult sermon for me to deliver because so many in the congregation were in the Navy. Just as I finished the sermon a woman stood who seemed to have been taken over by some transcendental power. With her eyes closed and her face turned heavenward she declared in a bold but very strange voice: "Hear this servant of mine. He comes with truth for you. His words are not his but mine. Hear him!"

When she finished there were moans and groans of "Thank you, Jesus" all over the congregation. Supposedly, God had spoken through her. I did not know what to make of her or her message. I was a bit shaken by it all. And I was even more concerned when I learned that the following day a young ensign resigned his commission in the Navy as a direct result of that sermon and prophecy.

Singing in the Spirit

One last thing to be defined that is high on the list of Pentecostal practices is what is called "singing in the Spirit." The Apostle Paul mentions this singing in 1 Corinthians 14:15: "What is it then? I will pray with the spirit, and I will pray with the understanding also: I will sing with the spirit, and I will sing with the understanding also."

When modern Pentecostals tell of singing in the Spirit they are talking about a practice that I have enjoyed and appreciated ever since I first encountered it. It is a form of worship in which a group of Christians sings praises to God, each individual in his or her own unique manner.

Some years ago some of my students invited me to go to a Saturday night charismatic prayer meeting that was being held at a Presbyterian church in Parkersford, Pennsylvania. After a few regular hymns the pastor instructed us to sing in the Spirit. "To do this," he said, "all you have to do is sing out words of praise to God to a tune that you yourself make up. The Lord will do the rest."

Though I was hesitant, I gradually joined the rest of the congregation and carried out the pastor's instructions. More than two hundred of us each made up his or her own song of praise. Each sang simultaneously with the others. My own song had no rhyme to it. It was made up of phrases that came into my mind as I thought of the goodness and greatness of God. I sang these words to notes that came to me as I went along. Others did the same.

Instead of the confusing array of noises that I had expected to hear, I found that all of these individual songs of praise blended into the most ethereal, melodious music I have ever heard. The beauty of it affected me so much that I stopped my own "singing in the Spirit" just so that I might take in more fully the music that filled the sanctuary. This was a part of the Pentecostal movement that I very much appreciated.

Since the modern Pentecostal movement is dynamic and in flux there will be new terms and new definitions needed in the years to come. But this brief survey of some of the most common features of the Charismatic movement should provide those who are on the outside some idea of what Pentecostals are talking about and how their particular practices work themselves out in the life of the church of the twentieth century.

The Working Presence of the Spirit

Chapter 4

Romans 8:
The Pentecostal
Movement

Those of us who do not belong to Pentecostal churches often are not sufficiently aware of what can be called the "now work" of Jesus. We in the evangelical tradition are constantly preaching and teaching what Jesus did for us *two thousand years ago* on the cross. Furthermore, we spend much time and energy exploring how the life that Jesus lived out here on earth exemplifies personal morality and social justice for those who live today. But so much of what concerns us in the church has to do with the historical Jesus. We are sometimes guilty of confining becoming a Christian to accepting by faith what was accomplished for us in the remote past. In all of this we prove to minimize what the resurrected Jesus wants to do *to* us and *with* us *now* through the ministry of the Holy Spirit. This is what can be referred to as the *now work* of Christ. And this latter emphasis on what Jesus effects in the lives of Christians in the here and now should be a primary concern of Christians whether they call themselves Pentecostals or not.

Being Christian is not just believing in some propositional statements about a man whom the church says was God. It is not only accepting the good news that two thousand years ago Jesus absorbed our sin on a cross and endured the punishment for it

47

that we deserve. It is much more than that. Being a Christian involves something *happening* to us in the *now*. It is linked to an intensely personal relationship with Christ in our everyday lives. Each of us should be able to testify to being aware of a mystical presence that enlivens us, convinces us we are loved, leads us, directs us, and strengthens us to live out the will of God. Each of us should be experiencing an indwelling presence that enables us to taste a special joy and a love that is difficult to describe to anybody who isn't familiar with the same kind of experience. Because of what Jesus is doing in us now, each of us should be evidencing a change in personality whereby the fruit of the Spirit—love, joy, peace, long-suffering, gentleness, goodness, faith, meekness, temperance—are increasingly obvious to others.

Being Christian, therefore, is transrational. It involves ecstasy. It should provide a surge of psychic energy through which the deadness of the soul is vanquished. It should generate a glorious awareness of God's goodness in our lives.

It is this "now work" of Christ in the life of Christians that is specifically what theologians refer to as the ministry of the Holy Spirit. All Christians, not just those who call themselves Pentecostals, should be able to give testimonies of this ministry in their lives. All of us who call ourselves "born again" should be able to have something to say about being invaded by the Spirit and being made into the new persons that God wants us to be. Consequently, all Christians, whether or not they want anything to do with Pentecostalism or the Charismatic movement, should be able to talk about being filled with the Holy Spirit and about enjoying the fruits of a new life in Christ. In this sense we all ought to be able to talk about being Spirit-filled Christians even if we have no interest in speaking in tongues.

Nowhere in the Bible do we get a better overview of this now work of Christ than in the eighth chapter of Romans. There the work of the Holy Spirit is outlined in such a comprehensive manner that it is essential for us to give some extended attention to how that chapter spells out for us what the Holy Spirit does to us and for us as we surrender to His ministries. For our consideration I have broken the list down to the following:

1. Delivers us from defeatist attitudes.
2. Changes the way we think.
3. Gives us new enthusiasm about life.
4. Helps us make decisions.
5. Gives us a feeling of being close to God.
6. Gives us assurance that we are "saved."
7. Establishes a special closeness with God.
8. Defines a new and urgent mission for every Christian.
9. Works to save Planet Earth.
10. Guarantees us that God will triumph in history.

Let's look at each of these ministries one by one.

Delivers Us from Defeatist Attitudes

There is therefore now no condemnation to them which are in Christ Jesus, who walk not after the flesh, but after the Spirit. For the law of the Spirit of life in Christ Jesus hath made me free from the law of sin and death. For what the law could not do, in that it was weak through the flesh, God sending his own Son in the likeness of sinful flesh, and for sin condemned sin in the flesh: That the righteousness of the law might be fulfilled in us, who walk not after the flesh, but after the Spirit.

Romans 8:1–4

Romans 8 begins with the good news that there is no condemnation for those who are in Christ Jesus. That means that our righteous God, who by His nature must condemn sin wherever He finds it, will not punish us. This is because our sin has been transferred to Jesus who, in our place, has accepted the punishment that was our due. But there is even more to this verse than that. I believe that Paul is telling us that in Christ Jesus there is also an end to the *self*-condemnation that we all feel when we fail to live up to the demands of our religious and family upbringing.

Standards have been set and expectations have been established for each and every one of us, but they seem to be more than we can handle. Our parents, our churches, and even our friends have built into our consciences a set of rules and expectations that we are supposed to live up to in our daily lives. Concepts of right and wrong are drummed into our heads as we are socialized into adulthood so that we cannot help but judge ourselves negatively as we fail to measure up to these internalized rules of life. Consequently, most of us end up feeling like failures, suffering from guilt complexes, and having low self-esteem. In our everyday behavior we find that we violate our consciences and fail to live up to what we think we are supposed to be. We end up being down on ourselves for our inability to be as good as our superegos tell us we should be and as decent as we think those around us expect us to be. The result is that we suffer depression. And in extreme cases some of us hate ourselves so much that we become suicidal.

In the opening verse of Romans 8 Paul explains that this condition is universal. Everybody cannot help but feel condemned. We all will find that we suffer from a sense of being disgusted with ourselves.

Some us of us try to compensate for these feelings by becoming overachievers. We try to tell ourselves that if we just can do enough good it will certainly outweigh the sins we have committed. Some of us drive ourselves to try to accumulate an impressive load of good deeds. But try as we may and regardless of what we accomplish we still suffer from the inner anguish of self-condemnation.

Down deep inside we have this image of God holding a set of scales. On the one side is piled all the evil we have done and on the other side is all the good. We keep telling ourselves that we will be okay if we can just pile up enough good things to outweigh the bad. But the bad news is that this solution, though often tried, never works.

When Bible-thumping revivalists try to lay a guilt trip on us I feel like saying, "Don't bother, we already feel guilty enough." Romans 8 tells us that "the flesh" is weak, and our own experiences verify this fact.

But over and against this condemnation, there is good news. Whereas the laws of God as laid down in the Bible declare us guilty, on the one hand, and our consciences lead us to self-condemnation, on the other, all of that is overcome by what Jesus can do for us through the Holy Spirit. The deadly effects of condemnation can be completely wiped out of our lives in the here and now. Through the Holy Spirit we can be mystically connected to Christ on the cross, and all that is wrong with us can be drained from us and transferred over to the dying Jesus. In this passage Paul is telling us the fantastic news that Jesus will free us from the deadly effects of God's condemnation and our own self-condemnation if we are willing to submit to the Holy Spirit.

Anybody who knows anything about counseling knows about the principle of transference. The good counselor becomes so emotionally empathetic with the client that the counselor feels what the client feels. The counselor feels the client's psychological pain so deeply that, little by little, that pain is absorbed by the counselor. By the end of the session the client is likely to feel much better, but the counselor is likely to feel terrible. What has happened is that the counselor has taken upon himself what is wrong with the client. The pain and suffering that was once a burden to the client have been transferred to the counselor.

A really good counselor will find counseling exhausting, because it takes a great deal of psychic strength to endure that kind of punishment.

This, in a sense, is the ministry of the Holy Spirit. He connects us to the Ultimate Counselor—Jesus Christ. The Holy Spirit enables us to be in Christ and for Christ to be in us. The Holy Spirit makes it possible for all the ugly, painful realities of our guilt and condemnation to be transferred to the crucified Jesus. It is the Spirit that gives validity to the prophet Isaiah who says to us, "Surely he hath borne our griefs, and carried our sorrows" (Isa. 53:4).

We must cooperate if this miraculous deliverance from condemnation is to be enjoyed. Each of us must believe the good news of the gospel and then yield to what the Holy Spirit wants to do to us. Each of us must be willing to let the Holy Spirit connect us to the transforming presence of the crucified Christ. What I am suggesting is that each of us must allow time each day to be surrendered to the ministry of the Holy Spirit as He unites us with the Christ who saves.

In my own life I go through the process of yielding to what the Holy Spirit wants to accomplish in me when I am lying in bed. Often in the night, I lie back and call upon the Spirit to unite me with Christ who, in turn, drains from me all that is negative and evil. I surrender and yield to all that the Spirit wants to accomplish in me by placing me in Christ and placing Christ in me. I let the Spirit link me to the Jesus of history and deliver me from all that I despise about myself. Because of the work of the Spirit I no longer have to feel guilty over my inability to live up to the demands of God and the demands of my conscience. I don't have to go on being hard on myself by trying to make myself "good enough" for God. The ministry of the Holy Spirit sets me free from all of that. There is no condemnation for those who, through the Spirit, are in Christ Jesus.

Changes the Way We Think

For they that are after the flesh do mind the things of the flesh; but they that are after the Spirit the things of the Spirit. For to be carnally minded is death; but to be spiritually minded is life and peace. Because the carnal mind is enmity against God: for it is not subject to the law of God, neither indeed can be. So then they that are in the flesh cannot please God. But ye are not in the flesh, but in the Spirit, if so be that the Spirit of God dwell in you. Now if any man have not the Spirit of Christ, he is none of his.

Romans 8:5–9

Some sociologists call it an "alteration of consciousness." Some psychologists call it "behavioral modification." But in the simple and profound words of the Apostle Paul, the ministry of the Holy Spirit is a ministry that changes the way we think and, more specifically, what it is that we want out of life.

Sigmund Freud said that human beings, by nature, are creatures whose basic desire is to have their sexual hungers gratified. There is truth in Freud's assessment of human nature.

Frederick Nietzsche, the existentialist philosopher, had what I believe was an even more inclusive interpretation of human nature as he claimed that at the base of every person's psyche was a "will to power." The will to power, according to Nietzsche, involved the desire to dominate others sexually, but it also included the will to achieve power over others by such means as gaining social status and accumulating wealth.

The Apostle Paul would not have argued with either of these descriptions of human nature. He would simply contend that all such behavior was "living after the flesh" and would label such thought and motivations as natural for those with "carnal minds." Paul would not have been at odds with the insights of these modern psychologists and philosophers. It is just that he would claim that we do not have to remain in this psychological condition and state of being. We can be changed, he would argue. And bringing about this change in us is the work of the Holy Spirit. That is what he tried to tell us in Romans 8:5–9.

When I was a kid my mother was always concerned about whom I chose to be my friends. She was always checking to find out what they talked about and how they thought. My mother was convinced that my friends would strongly influence how I thought and what I did.

In a sense Paul is urging each of us to have a personal relationship with Christ through the Holy Spirit so that little by little we might take on the mind of Christ (Phil. 2:5). He urges us to be intensely related to Christ through the Spirit so we will gradually come to think and feel as Christ does about things.

Two thousand years ago Jesus chose twelve men to walk with Him and talk with Him day in and day out. What transpired between Jesus and those men altered their way of thinking and modified their way of life. Paul believes that through the Holy Spirit that same Jesus can be with each of us in a personal way. Through the Holy Spirit, Paul contends, each of us can experience a closeness with Jesus and, in that closeness, be changed by Him into what He is. The Holy Spirit makes the resurrected Jesus contemporaneous with us. Through the Holy Spirit we are made to *feel* Jesus walking with us and talking to us.

It is in this context that Albert Schweitzer, in spite of his rational skepticism, wrote:

> He comes to us as One unknown, without a name, as of old, by the lake-side, He came to those men who knew Him not. He speaks to us the same word: "Follow thou me!" and sets us to the tasks which He has to fulfill for our time. He commands. And to those who obey Him, whether they be wise or simple, He will reveal Himself in the toils, the conflicts, the sufferings which they shall pass through in His fellowship, and, as an ineffable mystery, they shall learn in their own experience Who He is.

In my own life I find that having my mind and heart changed through the work of the Holy Spirit requires that I take time to be alone, and in that aloneness I must ask the Holy Spirit to make Jesus real to me. In such moments I plead for the Holy Spirit to do what I cannot do through any kind of psychic manipulations or thought processes that I can control. Instead I must plead, in the words of the Apostle Paul, "That I may know him, and the power of his resurrection, and the fellowship of his sufferings, being made conformable unto his death" (Phil. 3:10). To experience the ministry of the Holy Spirit, I wait patiently on the Lord (Ps. 40:1). I must wait for the presence of Christ made real to me through the Spirit. I must wait for a sense of nearness. At such times I do not pray for any *thing*. I simply pray for Him. I wait for the Spirit to fill me with His thinking and with His feelings. I try to patiently wait for the Holy Spirit to bring Christ and me together and to give me the feeling of oneness with Him. It is out of such experiences that I can sense the sentiment that lies behind that old favorite gospel song, "In the Garden."

> I come to the garden alone,
> While the dew is still on the roses;
> And the voice I hear,
> Falling on my ear,
> The Son of God discloses . . .

As Dietrich Bonhoeffer suggests so eloquently in his book *Life Together*, only those who meet Him in this kind of aloneness will be able to be aware of Him when they are with others.

Through the ministry of the Holy Spirit, Jesus changes us. The changes in personhood that the Spirit makes possible do not occur all at once. It takes a lifetime of practicing His presence, and then some, before the full impact of the relationship can be realized. Those who believe that immediately after a conversion experience all "dirty thoughts" of preconversion days will be gone and everything about their lives will be purity and light are in for disillusionment. But to those who ask the Holy Spirit to make Jesus real to them and to those who are willing to "wait patiently for the Lord," there is an inevitable change in thinking and feeling. The carnal dies out little by little and a new consciousness gradually emerges. The Apostle Paul readily admitted that he was still in such a process throughout his entire life (Phil. 3:13–14). He assumed that in his earthly lifetime he would never be completely in sync with the mind of Christ. That is what he believed eternity is for.

Gives Us New Enthusiasm About Life

> But ye are not in the flesh, but in the Spirit, if so be that the Spirit of God dwell in you. Now if any man have not the Spirit of Christ, he is none of his. And if Christ be in you, the body is dead because of sin; but the Spirit is life because of righteousness. But if the Spirit of him that raised up Jesus from the dead dwell in you, he that raised up Christ from the dead shall also quicken your mortal bodies by his Spirit that dwelleth in you.
>
> *Romans 8:9–11*

Pentecostals do have more fun. Those of us who belong to non-Pentecostal denominations have to admit that their worship services have a spontaneity and an aliveness to them that sometimes generates envy among us. Their exuberance often proves contagious and has a way of getting us enthusiastically involved. But being Spirit-filled provides much more than just a quality of excitement about worship. The Holy Spirit provides dynamism for all of life. In Romans 8:11 we read that it is this life-generating force that once infused the corpse of the dead Jesus and brought Him back to life again. The Spirit, says

Paul, can be a miraculous presence in us as contemporary Christians and into whomever He flows; the Spirit creates vitality.

As a kid I always loved those Frankenstein movies in which some mad scientist hooked electrodes up to a corpse, threw a switch and generated new life. Of course, the mystery surrounding the resurrection of Jesus infinitely transcends any such crude comparison. However, the Bible does suggest that the Holy Spirit is the energy that gave life back to the crucified and buried Jesus and that this same Spirit can infuse us with life, both now and after death.

From the moment we are born we begin to die. The power of death is at work in us from the moment we begin to breathe. All during life we fight against death, but it is a losing struggle. In the end, death claims us all. However, for those of us who surrender to the infilling of the Holy Spirit, there is a countervailing energy at work that wars against death. In the end, when death appears to have won and has laid us in the grave, this life-giving force reverses everything and brings us back to life. It is this incredible miracle wrought by the Spirit that prompts the Apostle Paul to declare "O death, where is thy sting? O grave, where is thy victory?" (1 Cor. 15:55).

Paul also wants us to know that we do not have to wait until death to experience the regenerating ministry of the Holy Spirit. Even in our present lives, if we surrender to the infilling of the Spirit, we can experience an exhilarating force vibrating through us. It is a ministry of the Holy Spirit to drive the deadness of our souls away and to banish the apathy that infects most other people. The Spirit can create an aliveness and a vitality that expels the boring dullness of the mundane forever.

The craving for the enlivening infilling of the Spirit lay behind the hymn, "Spirit of God, Descend Upon My Heart." The memorable second verse reads:

57

I ask no dream, no prophet ecstasies,
No sudden rending of the vale of clay,
No angel visitant, no op'ning skies;
But take the dimness of my soul away.

Ups and Downs in the Spirit

From all of this talk about the aliveness in the Spirit, one might conclude that those who are surrendered to the Holy Spirit live in some kind of perpetual euphoria. When people give their testimonies about being Spirit-filled, they often give this impression and leave the rest of us who have our ups and downs feeling somewhat inferior. In reality those who have had charismatic experiences are also likely to have depressions and down times. But (and this is a big 'but') there is a major difference in the emotional state of those who are Spirit-filled as opposed to those who are not. To illustrate this difference, I would like for you to imagine going with me to Haiti, where some of my friends serve as missionaries.

The roads in Haiti are very bad. Once our truck leaves the main highway, we find ourselves bouncing up and down. The ruts and bumps keep us in perpetual motion.

As the road winds north, however, toward the city of Cap-Haitien, it leads us into the mountains. Just a couple of hours after leaving the capital of Port-au-Prince, we find ourselves several thousand feet above sea level. Up there in the mountains the roads prove to be even worse, and we continue to find ourselves bouncing up and down more than ever. But note this—when we are up there in the mountains, even when we are down, we are still thousands of feet higher than when we were *up* while we were *down* at sea level. (You may need spiritual discernment to make your way through what I just said.) By analogy, I am saying that the Spirit-filled Christian has down times, but the down times are still much higher than the up times that characterize life before the charismatic infilling.

On a personal level, I would not trade the down times that I have known since being surrendered to the Holy Spirit for the up times that I used to know before then. Being alive in the Spirit is not a deliverance from ups and downs, but it certainly is an opportunity to live life on a whole new level.

Chapter 5

More About Romans 8

All of the dimensions of spirituality that we have been cover-
ing in our reading of Romans 8 involve ministries of the Holy
Spirit that every growing Christian should want to experience.
You do not have to be a Pentecostal gifted with an ability to pray
in another tongue to want the kinds of blessings that we have
been talking about here. When being filled with the Spirit is put
into proper perspective, I have to say that speaking and praying
in tongues is only a small part of what the charismatic experience
is all about. Given the choice, if a choice had to be made, between having the gift of tongues and having all of the other great
things that Romans 8 tells us that the Spirit can give us, probably
every Pentecostal I know would decide to give up on tongues for
these other blessings. And there is more.

The Spirit Helps Us to Make Decisions

Every day is filled with decisions and at times it is hard to figure
out just what is the right thing to do. Sometimes the decisions we

have to make are of such significance that we know mistakes could mess up the rest of our lives. Decisions such as who to marry, what vocational choices to make, and what kind of lifestyle to adopt can fix our destinies more than we want to admit. But even decisions that may seem relatively insignificant at the time we are making them, in retrospect, can turn out to have awesome consequences. If we stop to think about it, we readily realize the immense burden that the freedom to choose proves to be. For many, it is a burden too heavy to bear alone.

Young people often are immobilized by the decision-making process. If, as they are finishing high school, you were to ask them what they planned to do after graduation, you probably would be greeted by a shrug of the shoulders and an almost moronic "I dunno." If you then send them on to college and, after four years and a lot of money, ask them the same question again, you still probably would get "I dunno"—unless, of course, you send them to those elite institutions of higher learning. In that case they probably would answer, "I am keeping all of my options open."

With such confusion about what to do and what decisions to make, it is good news to hear that one of the primary ministries of the Holy Spirit is to provide guidance for those of us who want it. Romans 8:14 tells us that the Holy Spirit will lead us in the decision-making process if we want Him to. Furthermore, this verse tells us that only those who are willing to be led by the Holy Spirit in their daily decision-making can really call themselves "the children of God."

The Spirit Leads One Day at a Time

I am often with college students when I am out on the speaking circuit. And the most common question they ask me is, "How can I discover the will of God for my life?"

I always answer, "You can't! It does not work that way." Then I go on and give them this illustration to make my point.

64

"There are two ways that I can tell you how to get from here to Eastern College where I teach. I can give you a map that charts out the route for you to take. With such a map you might or might not get there, depending on how good you are at reading maps.

"The other option I can offer is to get into your car, sit beside you, and direct you as we go along. In the latter case you might not have a complete idea of just how we are going to get to Eastern College, but you probably would have more confidence that you will get there. Being guided by somebody who knows the way is always superior to a map that is subject to being misread."

I then go on to explain to the students that there is a parallel here as to how the Holy Spirit guides us in our daily lives. God could provide us with a mapped-out scheme of the rest of our lives and then leave us on our own to follow those instructions, or He could send the Holy Spirit to travel along with us and guide us each step and turn along the way. Obviously, God in His goodness has chosen the latter and better way.

In John 14:15–18 Jesus told His disciples that they would always have the Holy Spirit with them. The word for the Holy Spirit that Jesus utilized on this occasion is the word "Comforter." A more modern translation out of the Greek language for this word could be "Co-pilot."

Jesus promised that the Holy Spirit would be with us as we move through life. This perfect Co-pilot will direct us and give us guidance. The Holy Spirit, according to the promise of Jesus, will always be there to show us the way through the confusing morass of decisions that threaten to undo us. Being Spirit-filled is having the assurance that our lives are under the control of One who knows what He is doing.

Gives Us Assurance That We Are Saved

The Spirit itself beareth witness with our spirit, that we are the children of God.

Romans 8:16

Getting assurance of salvation has long been a major concern of Christians. Most of us go through times when we wonder whether or not we might have been a bit too optimistic about our eternal destiny. Sometimes such doubts overwhelm us. This is particularly likely to happen if we find ourselves sitting under a high pressure evangelist who is desperate to get us down to the altar. A surefire line that can be used when he gives an invitation is to ask the congregation if they are "absolutely sure" of their salvation. This probing question is usually followed up with the line: "If you were to die tonight, are you certain, beyond a shadow of a doubt, that you would wake up tomorrow in heaven? If not, why not come forward tonight and be sure?"

To those of us who are susceptible to such manipulations, a tremor is sent up and down our spines. If we were not feeling doubt before, the evangelist is more than able to get our uncertainties into high gear with his questioning. We know that we can never be too sure, and we can find ourselves on the sawdust trail just so as to not take any chances.

Sören Kierkegaard, the Danish theologian/philosopher, once made the point that a certain amount of uncertainty is good in any relationship, including our relationship with God. Some doubt, contends Kierkegaard, keeps us on our toes. It keeps us from spiritual neglect and carelessness.

Any young person with any dating experience understands what Kierkegaard was talking about. A girl knows that if a guy gets "too sure" of her, she might not get treated too well. A guy, on the other hand, knows that if his sweetheart is too certain that he is "in the bag," she might begin to take him for granted. This consequence of sureness, contends Kierkegaard, is part of what lies behind "the hiddenness of God." A certain degree of concealment and uncertainty, he argues, makes us more careful about how we treat Him. The right kind of uncertainly can cause us to "take heed lest we fall" (1 Cor. 10:12).

There is a downside to doubt. There comes a point when uncertainty can become psychological torture. Kierkegaard himself knew all too well that such can be the case. His own existence was full of a debilitating and destructive kind of doubt. He constantly brooded over the painful question of whether or not God would ultimately condemn him. He was driven by a sense that he somehow had committed the unforgivable sin. Kierkegaard was not a happy man.

It is this latter destructive kind of doubt that the Holy Spirit seeks to drive from our lives. When such doubts and fears about my salvation overtake me, I can go to prayer and simply ask that the Holy Spirit remove them. The giving of assurance is a major part of the Spirit's ministry to us, and I simply surrender myself to Him so that He can do for me what I cannot do for myself.

What usually happens when I yield to the Spirit is that He brings passages of Scripture to my mind that give me the confidence that overcomes doubt. The objective truth revealed in the Bible is usually the instrument that the Spirit employs to drive away my subjective uncertainties and fears. Of all the passages that the Spirit brings to mind at such times, none seems to be of more help than the last verses of the eighth chapter of Romans:

> For I am persuaded, that neither death, nor life, nor angels, nor principalities, nor powers, nor things present, nor things to come, nor height, nor depth, nor any other creature, shall be able to separate us from the love of God, which is in Christ Jesus our Lord.
>
> *Romans 8:38–39*

The Spirit Establishes a Special Closeness with God

Once when a friend of mine told me that she was not satisfied with her relationship with God, I responded by telling her that nobody is. To be a Christian is always to want more than one has in the ways of closeness and depth of relationship with God. By nature we all have a hunger for God that cannot be fully satiated until that day comes when we are with Him in eternity. In a sense, this life involves purifying ourselves, growing in spiritual stature so that we will be as prepared as possible for that great encounter "beyond the bar" (1 John 3:2–3). The good news is that what will "be" can be partially tasted in the here and now. Even now each of us can personally experience a closeness with God that we hitherto might have thought impossible, regardless of how much we might have yearned for it. And it is the Holy Spirit who makes this happen.

To be filled with the Spirit is to possess a presence of God that is intensely personal. It is to have a soft, still voice in the depths of our being that whispers to us that we are more than saved. The Spirit convinces us that we are the sons and daughters of God.

Through the Spirit we can feel such a closeness with God that we can actually call God "Daddy." This relationship, as it is discussed by the Apostle Paul in Romans 8:15, was so awesome to the King James translators of the Bible that they left the word "Abba" untranslated. But scholars agree that "Abba" should have been translated "Daddy." It is a shame that it was not. That translation would have helped us all to understand in a fuller way what the Holy Spirit accomplished in the way of establishing a new relationship with God for those who want to receive it.

Being Italian, my son and I relate to each other in a somewhat special way. When we meet it is usually with hugs and kisses. There is little formality in our greetings, and there is no evidence of social distance. I'm his "Dad!" The truth is that he usually calls me "Pop!"

I explain all of this because it is clear from Romans 8 that, through the Holy Spirit, God is establishing an even more intimate and intensely personal relationship with His people than exists between my son and me. All concepts of God that view Him as some kind of transcendental Shylock demanding His pound of flesh must be abandoned. Through the Holy Spirit our God becomes our "Abba."

I have a friend who, when he has some time on his hands, loves to say to God over and over again, "Daddy, I love you!" He tells me that there is nothing magical or mystical about his simple words. He explains, "It just makes me feel good talking to Him that way."

A New and Urgent Mission for Every Christian

For the creature was made subject to vanity, not willingly, but by reason of him who hath subjected the same in hope, because the creature itself also shall be delivered from the bondage of corruption into the glorious liberty of the children of God. For we know that the whole creation groaneth and travaileth in pain together until now. And not only they, but ourselves also, which have the firstfruits of the Spirit, even we ourselves groan within ourselves, waiting for the adoption, to wit, the redemption of our body.

Romans 8:20–23

As the Holy Spirit gives direction to our individual lives, He simultaneously integrates us into God's grand mission to establish His Kingdom in this world. The Holy Spirit is a revolutionary force in society. It is the Holy Spirit working in us that turns us into persons who are set to work rescuing God's lost creation from its messed-up and polluted condition. If we read this scripture rightly, we cannot help but be impressed with the declaration that a truly Spirit-filled Christian will be involved in social action. The Spirit, according to these verses, motivates us to reverse the trends we see all around, toward aiding ecological recovery and toward transforming the structures of our society into institutions that reflect the justice of God. This same Spirit constrains us to convert the social institutions of our society so that they express more of the justice of the One who created them.

As a university student I had a hard time relating to the social movements evident on campus. Everywhere I turned during the early 1960s there were demonstrations and protest rallies conducted by those who were committed to ending racism, curtailing war, and abolishing poverty. These all were good causes, but they seemed to be detached from what the church was teaching about being spiritual. So far as I could grasp then, becoming spiritual was essentially an inner or subjective process through which the Spirit would sanctify me for the time when I would stand before the throne of God. It was studying these verses that convinced me that there was much more to being spiritual than that. This passage makes clear that God's purposes for this world includes remaking His creation into what He meant it to be when He first created it. It clearly states that to be spiritual is to surrender to the Holy Spirit and allow Him to make us into instruments through whom God can carry out this mission.

Most evangelical Christians have been sensitized to the biblical imperative for social action. We have overcome the fear of being labeled Social Gospelers and have attempted to propagate a wholistic gospel that will deliver humanity from sin, both on the personal and societal levels. Furthermore, we have come to see that social justice cannot be achieved in a simplistic fashion. We know that individualistic repentance for racism among church people will not automatically end discrimination, nor will the adoption of a simple lifestyle by a small fraction of the total church of Christ create a redistribution of wealth that will eliminate hunger in Third World countries.

Like most Evangelicals, I believed that justice would not roll down without structural change. Having been touched by the Marxist implications of Liberation Theology, I felt that only a radical restructuring of the economic institutions of the capitalistic world would facilitate the emergence of economic justice and social equality. I was convinced that institutions designed to make profits could not adequately and simultaneously meet human needs. Believing myself to be a God-ordained David, I looked for some corporate Goliath that I could fell with a single shot. I decided that my "prophetic" energies would be directed at the multinational corporation conglomerate, Gulf and Western.

I selected this company for a variety of reasons. First of all, the news media had already listed it among the "terrible ten" most responsible for exploitation in Third World countries. G&W was accused of taking vast amounts of land that should have produced food for the hungry and turning it to sugar production. A Chicago newspaper described the corporation's exploitation of Dominican laborers, and suits by the Securities and Exchange Commission accused the corporation of denying needed tax revenues to the Dominican Republic.

Second, the National Council of Churches had produced a filmstrip entitled *Guess Who's Coming to Breakfast*, which depicted G&W as one of those "principalities and powers" that deny Third World peasants just wages for their labor and the ability to determine their own destiny. Last, a decade of involvement in missionary work in the Dominican Republic had brought me into contact with a host of critics, particularly in that country's universities, who sincerely believed that G&W was responsible for the economic woes of the nation.

Attacking a large corporation is much easier than people suppose. Some friends and I secured a few shares of stock in Gulf and Western. This entitled us to go to stockholders' meetings and confront both executives and major shareholders with the nature of their sin. We were committed to admonishing them biblically and to calling these people to corporate repentance. We were not the first to take such action. The Division of Corporate Responsibility of the National Council of Churches and an order of

Roman Catholic nuns, the Adrian Sisters, had already gained permission to speak out for social justice at the stockholders' meeting.

We were contacted by Gulf and Western executives almost immediately after launching our attack, and they wanted to discuss with us our perception of their company's activities in the Dominican Republic. We traveled to New York determined to confront with the Word of God these men whom we believed to be demonic agents of capitalistic oppression.

The parable of Jesus that seemed to articulate our beliefs is the one in which a man goes on a long trip and leaves his vineyard in the hands of some stewards. The stewards run the vineyard in an oppressive manner, causing the workers to suffer. The master responds to the news of this oppression by sending messengers to warn the unfaithful stewards so that they might repent and correct their ways. But the stewards do not listen to the messengers. Finally the owner sends his own son, whom the unfaithful stewards put to death. The parable ends with Jesus asking what the owner of the vineyard will do to the unfaithful stewards when he returns.

We believed that Gulf and Western Company was God's vineyard, and that the executives of Gulf and Western were unfaithful stewards who were oppressing the poor. We believed we were the messengers of God who had come to bring warnings from God, the owner. If these unjust stewards did not listen to us, we were prepared to inform them that one day soon the true owner of Gulf and Western would return, and He would punish them. In our arrogance, we assumed that we were speaking for God and that these corporate executives were enemies of the Almighty.

When engaging in a prophetic ministry it is all too easy for Christians to assume that they are the righteous and that those whom they attack are the ungodly. In reality we were enjoying our roles as prophets and were somewhat guilty of being on an ego trip. It was heady stuff to believe ourselves to be the instruments of God and the champions of the poor.

But what we found in the executive suites of Gulf and Western was not what we expected. Executives from the top echelon of the company heard us out, listened to our complaints, talked with us reasonably, and urged that we do two things before our next meeting. First, they wanted us to conduct our own research into the accusations that had been leveled at them by the press and the National Council of Churches. Second, they wanted us to propose concrete ways in which they might be able to facilitate positive social change in the Dominican Republic. They pointed out that if we came simply with accusations, there could be no progress, but if we came with concrete proposals as to how Gulf and Western might participate in helping the Dominican people, then they would work with us to turn those proposals into reality.

Our research embarrassed us. We found that while Gulf and Western did have vast tracts of land in sugar production, most of the soil that they were utilizing was of such low quality that it was not good for anything but growing sugar. We also discovered that if Gulf and Western withdrew from the Dominican Republic, that land would still be in sugar production because it was good for nothing else. Better quality soils, identified through comprehensive analysis programs, were already turned over to the production of food crops for local consumption or were being donated to the government for development of small farm and ranch cooperatives.

The Dominican government had placed a ceiling on wages for sugar cutters, and Gulf and Western was paying the maximum that the government would allow. We found that the company was engaged in extensive housing construction projects to provide improved living quarters for its workers, and that these facilities were vastly superior to what was generally available to those who work in the sugar industry. With technical assistance from the Community Medicine Department at Mount Sinai School of Medicine in New York, the company was developing plans for comprehensive health programs for both the urban and rural sections of the eastern region of the country. We found that the Loma Romana region around G&W in the Dominican Republic was enjoying the highest economic prosperity of any section of that country, primarily due to the economic conditions created by the presence of Gulf and Western.

While there may be theorists who attempt to point out the long-range benefits that could result from the nationalization of Gulf and Western's land, it is obvious that the short-term impact of the removal of this corporation would mean the end of the economic prosperity that characterizes the eastern portion of the country. Quite frankly, much that we discovered surprised us. And as we accepted the G&W proposal to come up with concrete proposals to help the people of the Dominican Republic, we were further surprised.

We had decided that one of the best opportunities to improve the lot of the Dominican people lay in the development of the new university in the city of Azua in the southwestern part of the country. The people of that city had contacted me and asked for my help in developing a school that would provide leadership for the upgrading of the southwestern part of the nation. A vast irrigation system had just been completed in their region, making hundreds of thousands of acres suddenly available for cultivation. There was a need to train workers in the skills of farming. The land around Azua, unlike the sugar land in the eastern part of the country, was Grade "A" soil according to a United Nations study. Its quality and vastness gave this region of the country the opportunity of becoming a bread basket for the entire nation. Azua also had a need for people trained to be school teachers, paramedics, and technicians.

Our little group, which was incorporated as the Evangelical Association for the Promotion of Education, had provided consultant help for the development of what is now the Technical University of the South. We helped the people of Azua to develop a faculty, recruit students, secure building facilities, and buy the necessary equipment. Needless to say, our greatest problem in developing the new university had been to secure adequate funding. The initial money had come from individual evangelical Christians and their churches. A second source had been a grant from Rotary International. But much more was needed if the project was to succeed, and this was the concrete proposal presented to G&W.

The corporation's response was immediate and positive. Corporate executives not only visited the city Azua to encourage community leaders in their project and worked diligently to secure a significant grant for the new university, but they also encouraged other organizations that could help us to supply support. We have expectations that this new university, which presently enrolls 150 students and has 1,500 young people preparing for entrance, will provide the leadership that will guide the southwestern part of the country through a period of economic growth and social improvement.

Executives of G&W have proposed a significant approach between church groups and corporations doing business in the Third World. They have suggested a meeting that would bring together major corporate executives and the leaders of major religious groups for the purpose of determining ways in which they might work together to use their combined resources to help the people of Latin America. In such a meeting, Latin American leaders would be able to communicate to both church and corporate executives the directions that they believe development should take in their nations. It would be possible for these meetings to initiate an era of progress that would bring about changes in the economic structure of countries in Latin America without violent revolution or Marxist takeover.

One day I received a telephone call from the executive offices of Gulf and Western. They wanted me to be among the first to know that afternoon that an announcement would be made which would commit Gulf and Western to spend up to $100 million for social and economic development in the Dominican

Republic. The expenditure of this money would result in the construction of more than two hundred schoolrooms, further development in the health programs carried on in conjunction with Mount Sinai School of Medicine, the construction of more than four thousand new homes, and the development of an agricultural program that would make people in the eastern part of the country self-sufficient in regard to the provision of food. When I went to class and announced the news to my students, they spontaneously rose and sang the Doxology.

The good news is that the Gulf and Western executives kept their word. Today the western part of the Dominican Republic stands in sharp contrast to the rest of the country. With the company's help, the city of San Pedro de Macoris boasts one of the finest universities in Latin America. A diversified economy was developed by Gulf and Western, and this has made it possible for most of the people in that part of the country to work in relatively high-paying industrial jobs. Something of the Kingdom of God was realized through the resources and leadership of this multinational corporation. The Spirit works in strange ways His wonders to perform.

I still question some things that Gulf and Western is doing in the Dominican Republic. For example, I doubt that the development of tourism is a good thing for the nation. It turns many Dominicans into bellhops and maids and funnels very little money into the Dominican Republic economy. Furthermore, I question the good that comes from allowing a nation to become overly dependent on the production of one crop such as sugar, especially when that crop yields a product that is not good for anyone's health.

While my theology of society has been significantly influenced by the recent theologians of Latin America, I have been forced by my research and personal experiences to redefine my beliefs so that they represent a more optimistic view of the potentialities of capitalistic institutions. I have come to view them more in the light of what Hendrik Berkhof says about such structures in his book, *Christ and the Powers*. He would label corporate structures as principalities and powers, which, according to the first chapter of Colossians, were created by God to serve His purposes in history. Berkhof would readily admit that these principalities and powers are in a fallen state along with the human race, and, in accord with the teachings of the third chapter of Colossians, they can be the enemies of God. This does not mean that Christians should seek to destroy these structures. Instead, they should believe that God is able to redeem them for His use and put them to work for His purposes, and they should also acknowledge that Christians can participate with Him to this end.

I have come to believe that Jesus calls us to confront the leaders of corporate structures with biblical demands for righteousness and that we should work for a response from these corporate leaders that would result in socioeconomic practices that create good for people in society. I believe that the 1990s will witness a resurgence of social activism such as was evident in the 1960s. Unlike the sixties, however, the target for social action will not be the political system, but rather economic institutions. This coming decade will be a time in which Christians demand corporate responsibility from business executives. In this crusade, it will be all too easy for us to be informed by the exciting Marxist theologies of Latin America and demand that all capitalistic structures be replaced with a socialistic system. However, I choose to follow the suggestion of Berkhof and view capitalistic institutions as principalities and powers in need of redemption. I believe that the eighth chapter of Romans tells us that these institutions are "groaning and in travail waiting for the sons of God" to help them serve the purposes for which they were created.

The changing of a multinational corporation into an instrument of blessing is something that is willed by God, and it is something that He equips us to do through His Spirit.

The Spirit Works to Save Planet Earth

Romans 8:20–23 also has particular significance in light of what is happening to our physical environment. Our modern forms of technology and industrialization have taken a heavy toll on God's creation, and a great deal must be done in the immediate future if we are going to have a healthy and beautiful habitation for the next generation.

Right now we are polluting the oceans at such a rate that we are killing off the plankton that live in their waters. Plankton are a vast but unseen array of ocean plant life that produce most of the oxygen we breathe. Jacques Cousteau and many other oceanographers have found that the destruction of plankton is already extensive. They warn that the very supply of the air we breathe will be curtailed if things don't change soon.

Spirit-filled people will stop this destruction of the oceans. They will become agents of God who work to end the dumping of garbage and industrial waste into the oceans. They will work to protect our source of oxygen. They will declare the oceans as belonging to the Lord and will work for ways to make humanity show reverence for them.

Our automobiles hourly pump incredible amounts of sulfur fumes into the atmosphere. These fumes rise and mix with moisture into a mild but still dangerous form of sulfuric acid. What happens next is that this acid comes down on us in the form of rain.

All over New England and eastern Canada there are ponds and lakes without fish or other living organisms. This acid rain has flowed into them and killed everything that had life. Spirit-filled Christians will work for legislation that will require the cutting back of automobile exhaust fumes and will not rest until factory fumes are no longer toxic.

Every day we are sending chlorohydrocarbons into the atmosphere that in turn are destroying the ionosphere. This may

78

sound like a bunch of high-sounding words that only concern pointy-headed intellectuals, but if we want to have a future for Planet Earth we all had better become acquainted with these terms and understand their significance for our everyday life. The destruction of the ionosphere by chlorohydrocarbons produced by carbons from exhaust fumes is making us vulnerable to the rays of the sun that cause skin cancer.

The Greenhouse Effect is another concern. So many exhaust gases are collecting in the upper levels of the atmosphere that they are trapping heat that ought to be radiating into outer space. Sunlight comes through the atmosphere and generates heat when it hits the surface of the earth. In the past that heat was able to rise and escape the earth's atmosphere and thus keep the planet from overheating. We now find that the layer of chlorohydrocarbons that we have generated and allowed to accumulate in the upper regions of the atmosphere are trapping the heat which in turn is causing an overall rise in the earth's temperature.

In time this heating process will melt ice on the polar caps, which then will cause the level of the oceans to rise. This in turn will cause world-wide flooding. Add this specter to the possibility that the rising temperatures will make many parts of the world too warm for human beings to live in comfort, and you will get a slight glimpse of the results of our ecological sins.

I have not even asked you to consider the environmental tragedies that are resulting from the destruction of the rain forests of Brazil or the frightening consequences related to our attempts to get rid of nuclear waste.

Enough has been said already to provide ample evidence that "the whole creation groaneth and travaileth in pain" waiting for the children of God to rescue it from its plight (Rom. 8:22). God wants to "make all things new." And through the Holy Spirit He wills to make us into a people who are committed to this mission.

Guarantees Us That God Will Triumph in History

For we are saved by hope: but hope that is seen is not hope: for what a man seeth, why doth he yet hope for? But if we hope for that we see not, then do we with patience wait for it. Likewise the Spirit also helpeth our infirmities: for we know not what we should pray for as we ought: but the Spirit itself maketh intercession for us with groanings which cannot be uttered. And he that searcheth the hearts knoweth what is the mind of the Spirit, because he maketh intercession for the saints according to the will of God. And we know that all things work together for good to them that love God, to them who are the called according to his purpose. For whom he did foreknow, he also did predestinate to be conformed to the image of his Son, that he might be the firstborn among many brethren. Moreover whom he did predestinate, them he also called: and whom he called, them he also justified: and whom he justified, them he also glorified.

Romans 8:24–30

The world scene is so confusing that none of us is quite sure how to pray for it (v. 26). When there's a presidential election, we can't be sure as to which candidate would be best, so we often pray, "Thy will be done!" When international issues ranging from the Middle East crisis to concerns about revolutions in Latin America arise, we have a hard time figuring out what the future has in store for the human race. It is hard to get the truth through the media, so our ignorance adds to our confusion.

In the midst of such a morass of social and political anomie we get the message from Romans 8 that we need not be concerned. According to these verses, even though we do not know what to pray for and how to pray, the Holy Spirit prays through us and for us. In some way that is beyond anybody's understanding, the Spirit can become a presence in us and pray the prayers through us that we would pray if we knew how.

Then comes the most positive note of this entire chapter. In Romans 8:28 we are assured that in the midst of all that is happening in this crazy mixed-up world, God is at work. In the end, He will make it all turn out good! We are given, in this famous verse, the assurance that history will be placed under His control and will be molded to His ultimate intentions. The last syllable of recorded time will not be a bang or a whimper. Instead, it will be the triumph of God's will and the answer to prayers that the Spirit prayed through us.

On the Personal Level with Romans 8:28

Most of us know Romans 8:28, and some of us can even recite it from memory. But in most cases we only apply the verse on the personal level. Of course the verse *does* have tremendous value when applied on the personal level. Each of us needs the assurance that even as we experience the painful and tragic events of life, God will have the last word and make things right.

Obviously, everything that happens is *not* God's will. The murder, child abuse, rape, and destruction that impact people's lives do not come from God. Scripture clearly states that God is not the author of evil (James 1:13, 17). What Romans 8:28 tells us is that God has a way of turning even demonically created tragedies into something positive. God is able to bring His good out of anything and everything.

Some years ago, when Jack Parr was the host of the "Tonight Show," America was regularly treated to the piano playing of Jose Mellis. Mellis, who was the music director for the show, regularly amazed the television audiences with his versatility on the keyboard.

One of the really fascinating things that Mellis would do was to invite Parr to come over to his piano and strike the keys in a completely arbitrary manner. Parr would strike a horrendous discord and then say to Mellis, "Okay, Jose, let's see what you can do with that."

Mellis would respond by putting his fingers on the keys struck by Parr and blend the notes of the discord into a beautiful piece of music. He would not only start with the discord struck by Parr, he would come back to it time and time again, making it an integral part of the music. Something ugly was transformed into something beautiful while America watched and listened.

I often thought, as I watched Jose Mellis perform his magic on the keyboard, that there was an analogy there to what God does. When we sin and mess up our lives, we strike discords. The demonic powers of the universe create tragedies. But God puts His fingers on the keys, takes those ugly discords, and blends them miraculously into His beautiful symphony of history.

When sin and evil hit us, when tragedy overtakes us, when sickness and accidents take away people whom we love, we dare not blame God. We dishonor Him if we make Him the cause of our suffering. Instead we can attribute the evil that befalls us to Satan and to those people who allow themselves to be his agents for evil. Then we can go on to announce the good news. Evil does not have the final word. God does. He will put His hands on the confusion and suffering that has come to pass and turn it all into something good. God, through His Spirit, is at work. He will accomplish His purposes. His will *will* be done on earth as it is in heaven. The Spirit is the driving force of history and that means we know how the battle of the ages ends—Jesus wins.

Chapter 6

How to Make It Happen

When Paul got to Ephesus he found a group of Christians there who already had heard and believed in the gospel. But when Paul asked them if they had received the Holy Spirit it was quite evident that they did not have the slightest idea in the world what he was talking about. They, like many of us, accepted the Good News that there had been a historical person named Jesus of Nazareth who had lived out the will of God, demonstrated a new way of life, had allowed Himself to be crucified in order to atone for their sins, had been resurrected from the grave three days later, and forty days after that had ascended into heaven. Paul found that the Ephesian Christians had a good theology, but he also found that they were lacking in the dynamism and joy that comes from being filled with the Holy Spirit.

And it came to pass, that, while Apollos was at Corinth, Paul having passed through the upper coasts came to Ephesus: and finding certain disciples, he said unto them, Have ye received the Holy Ghost since ye believed? And they said unto him, We have not so much as heard whether there be any Holy Ghost. And he said unto them, Unto what then were ye baptized? And they said, Unto John's baptism. Then said Paul, John verily baptized with the baptism of repentance, saying unto the people, that they should believe on him which should come after him, that is, on Christ Jesus. When they heard this, they were baptized in the name of the Lord Jesus. And when Paul had laid his hands upon them, the Holy Ghost came on them; and they spake with tongues, and prophesied.

Acts 19:1–6

What was missing were the effects of that mystical communion with the resurrected Jesus, which is what comes from what Pentecostals refer to as being filled with the Spirit.

Jesus is not just a historical fact. He is an abiding presence, and we can surrender to an intimate relationship with Him. Each of us can yield to a spiritual force that will bring us into oneness with Him.

Theology According to Star Trek

I always enjoy telling my students that my theology has been heavily influenced by the television series "Star Trek." In that series the viewers are indirectly taught a great deal about quantum physics and especially Einstein's theory of relativity. The spaceship *Enterprise* and its Starfleet crew are able to change their place in time simply by changing the speed at which they travel. The faster they go, the more they can move forward in time.

There is some truth in this setup because Albert Einstein theoretically established the claim that time and motion are relative to each other. According to Einstein, if we put you into a rocket ship and sent you into space at a 170,000 miles per second (relative to us) and gave you instructions to come back in 10 years, some very strange things would happen. If you marked off a day for every 24 hours of your time and a year for every 365 days and then returned 10 years later by your time, you would be astonished to find that the rest of us would be 20 years older. Traveling 170,000 miles per second relative to us, our 20 years, according to Einstein's theory, would pass in only 10 years of your time. As your speed approached the speed of light the process would be even more pronounced. At 180,000 miles per second, 20 years of our time might occur in one day of your time. And if you could travel at 186,000 miles per second, the speed of light, all of time would occur simultaneously. All events in human history would occur in the "now" for you.

The reason I took you on this brief excursion into quantum physics was to provide you with some help in grasping how the Jesus who was on the cross two thousand years ago can be contemporaneous with you in the here and now. Because Jesus is God, all things happen in the now for Him. Consequently, when He was on the cross two thousand years ago, He was contemporaneous with each of us every moment of every day of our lives. On the cross He is able to permeate our every experience and situation; from the cross He can transform us and impact what is happening to us. Jesus lived then and also lives in the now. That is why He could say, "Before Abraham was, I Am" (John 8:58). Being God, Jesus was able to experience that time which was before the ancient Hebrew patriarch as part of His now.

What all of this means to us is that in this present moment Jesus can relate to each of us from His cross two thousand years ago. From the cross, at this very instant, He can enter into each and every person and drain from us all the filth and sin that we have gleaned over the years. Like a sponge, He can absorb all that is dark and negative about us and make it His own. Jesus on the cross is our contemporary. Our "now" is His "now." And in this existential moment He can become the negative sinful persons we have been. He not only allows for our sin, He is able to become everything about each of us that is sinful. And He is able to do it this very moment—if we let Him.

It was His becoming sin that made Jesus literally sweat blood in the Garden of Gethsemane. It was not that He was afraid of dying. He knew that death would not be able to conquer Him. He knew that He would be resurrected. After all, he predicted His resurrection over and over again. He said that if they put Him in the grave He would return from the dead in three days (Mark 8:31). He told His detractors that if they tore down His body, in three days He would rebuild it (Mark 14:58). Death was no ultimate threat to Him.

He might have been hesitant about facing the pain of the cross, because crucifixion is one of the most torturous ways of dying. But I do not think that it was the fear of pain that led Him to pray to the Father that "this cup" might be taken from Him (Matt. 26:39). That is not why I think He pleaded for Plan B. It was, in all probability, His awareness that on the cross He would become contemporaneous with every sin and every sinner committing every sin. He knew that in His "eternal now" He would take all of that sin onto Himself and become what sin has made of each of us. "For he hath made him to be sin for us, who knew no sin; that we might be made the righteousness of God in him" (2 Cor. 5:21).

The good news is that at this very moment, even as you are reading this, you can let it happen. You can stop resisting what He wants to do for you and in you. You can allow Him to absorb the dark side of your personhood and drain the sin from your soul. The Holy Spirit wants to link you up to Him, even as He hangs on the tree. The Holy Spirit wants to connect you to his writhing body nailed obscenely to the Roman gibbet. All this can happen now.

This is not all! He not only absorbs all about each of us that is dark and sinful, but He will let all that is good and loving and beautiful about His personhood flow into us. Jesus on the cross is connected to us in the Holy Spirit so that *the great exchange* can take place. In the *now* our sin can be exchanged for His righteousness.

And he received the sign of circumcision, a seal of the righteousness of the faith which he had yet being uncircumcised: that he might be the father of all them that believe, though they be not circumcised; that righteousness might be imputed unto them also.

Romans 4:11

In the *now* He will exchange our troubled guilty state of consciousness for His joy and peace.

But he was wounded for our transgressions, he was bruised for our iniquities: the chastisement of our peace was upon him; and with his stripes we are healed.

Isaiah 53:5

The Christians at Ephesus had believed in the *objective* dimensions of the crucifixion. They knew that in the economy of the Heavenly Father they would not have to be punished for their sins because Jesus had been punished in their place. But what the Ephesian Christians had not encountered was this transforming involvement with Jesus on the cross in the "now." They had not experienced this *subjective* side of His salvation on the cross. The objective truth can be apprehended in the scriptures and can be cognitively grasped by anyone hearing the word of God. But the overpowering transformation in the "now" is the work brought about through the Holy Spirit. The Ephesian Christians, when Paul first met them, had accepted the former as truth. But they had not yet yielded to being personally possessed by Jesus.

Making It Happen

Of course all of this may still have you asking yourself, "But how do I make this happen? How can I get the Holy Spirit to connect me with the crucified Jesus in the now? How can I get to the cross and receive the blessings that are being described?"

The answer is both simple and difficult. It is simple in that the explanation of what has to be done is not at all complex. It is difficult in that what is required of the individual who wants this special relationship to happen may be the hardest thing any individual ever has been called upon to do. What is required is that you fully surrender yourself to whatever God wants to do to you. The infilling comes when you put no conditions on what you are willing to surrender in establishing a relationship with God. You must be ready to pray a prayer that goes something like this:

> Dear God, You can change me any way You want to change me. You can take out of me whatever You want to remove. If there are some relationships with certain people that You want me to end because they are sinful, I am ready to end them. If there are some sinful pleasures of the flesh that I have become addicted to, I am ready to be released from them and give them up. If there are feelings of lust and anger and envy and hate within me, I am willing to let them go.
>
> Dear God, You can send me wherever You want me to go, to do whatever You want me to do, to say whatever You want me to say, and to be whatever You want me to be. I am surrendered to Your will. Cleanse me, change me, and through your Holy Spirit help me to be in Christ and for Christ to be in me. Dear God, please baptize me in the Holy Spirit. Amen!

The Holy Spirit is already a presence in your life and is waiting to explode into radiant power throughout your entire personality. He is waiting for you to yield without reservation to what He wants to alter in your character. Up until the moment of full surrender you are "quenching" the Spirit. Until you say in the depths of your being, "I am ready and willing for You to take out of me whatever You want to remove and to direct me to do whatever You desire," you stifle the Spirit.

By maintaining control of your life and claiming self-mastery over your destiny you keep the lid on the Holy Spirit and frustrate His impact on your life. The only way to release His ministry in you is by making a conscious decision to yield to whatever He chooses to make of you.

There is just one other thing to be emphasized in this call to full surrender. It is your need for confession. If God is going to release the power of His Spirit within you, then you must be willing to confess the wrongs you have done, not only to God, but also to those you have hurt (Matt. 5:23–24). This means going to persons against whom you have sinned, telling them what you did, and asking for forgiveness. Unconfessed sin grieves the Spirit and keeps you from the joyful sense of release that God wants for you to enjoy. "If we confess our sins, he is faithful and just to forgive us our sins, and to cleanse us from all unrighteousness" (1 John 1:9).

Confessing to God is one thing, since you have biblical assurance that He will forgive you. But confessing to those whom you have hurt and wronged is quite another, since you can never be sure how they will react. Confessing can get you into a great deal of trouble. However, without confession it is difficult, if not impossible, to be reconciled to those whom sin has made into strangers. And without an honest effort to be reconciled with them there can be no reconciliation with God.

> Therefore if thou bring thy gift to the altar, and there rememberest that thy brother hath ought against thee; leave there thy gift before the altar, and go thy way; first be reconciled to thy brother, and then come and offer thy gift.
>
> *Matthew 5:23–24*

The sermons I heard as a child always left me believing that being at one with God was to precede being reconciled with other people. I can still hear my preacher explaining the cross as being composed of two wooden beams; one that was vertical and one that was horizontal. Then he would go on to explain that the vertical beam represented getting "right" with God. He claimed that only after that right relationship with God was established was there any hope of establishing the horizontal relationships in which we get right with others.

It made for an interesting sermon, but it was questionable theology. Obviously, Jesus put it the other way around. "Get right with your brothers and sisters before you come to the altar to meet God" is His command (Matt. 5:23–24). Being reconciled to those whom you have wronged is a precondition to having that sense of spiritual oneness with God.

Chuck Colson tells of taking a group of Christians into the Indiana State Penitentiary to minister to the inmates on death row. Following the evangelistic services, as the group was checking out of the prison, it was discovered that one of the group was missing. Along with a guard, Colson then hurried back to the death row cellblock to hunt for the missing person. What they found was the Christian worker in deep discussion with one of the prisoners.

Colson scolded the man. He let him know that he had jeopardized the relationship that this Christian ministry had established with the warden.

"You don't understand," was the answer. "This is James Brewer. He's condemned to die. I'm Judge Clement. I'm the one who sentenced him. Since that time we've both become Christians, and we need some time to confess and to forgive each other."

Unquestionably, in that cellblock something of the Day of Pentecost was re-experienced. There is no doubt that spiritual release took place. Confession is a precondition for the infilling of the Spirit.

J. Edwin Orr, a former professor of Church history at Fuller Theological Seminary, described the great outpouring of the Holy Spirit during the Welch Revivals of the nineteenth century. As people sought the infilling of the Spirit they did all they could to confess wrongdoings and to make restitution. This unexpectedly created severe problems for the shipyards along the coast of Wales. Over the years workers had pilfered all kinds of things. Everything from wheelbarrows to hammers had been stolen. However, as people sought to be right with God they started to return what they had taken, with the result that soon the shipyards of Wales were overwhelmed with returned property. There were such huge piles of returned tools that several of the yards had to put up signs that read, IF YOU HAVE BEEN LED BY GOD TO RETURN WHAT YOU HAVE STOLEN, PLEASE KNOW THAT THE MANAGEMENT FORGIVES YOU AND WISHES YOU TO KEEP WHAT YOU HAVE TAKEN.

A former student of mine recently returned to campus to be reconciled to a coed he had dated during his undergrad days. He had no intention of establishing a lasting relationship with her when he told her that he loved her. What he had said was only a ploy to get her to go to bed with him. Since then he had married another woman. But the guilt of what he had done haunted him, and he knew that he would never be able to experience the fullness of the Spirit in his life until he came back to campus and asked the woman he had wronged for forgiveness. This story does not have one of those happily-ever-after endings. The offended woman responded to his confession and plea by lashing out at him in furious anger.

It can be dangerous to confess. But it is necessary if you want to experience the infilling of the Holy Spirit.

A Word of Caution

There does have to be a cautionary note in this directive concerning confession. Specifically, you have to ask yourself whether or not the confession will do more harm than good. For instance, a man who had committed adultery with his friend's wife asked me if he should confess to his friend what had happened.

He told me that he had already straightened things out with his own wife but wondered whether or not he should clear things up with his friend. This man was earnestly seeking a deeper walk in the Spirit and wondered whether this confession was something he had to do.

I asked him how he thought the confession would affect the other couple. He explained that he thought that it would affect them greatly and might do irreparable harm to their relationship. My advice to him was to talk to the man's wife about it all, but in the end to leave it up to her to confess as she saw fit.

There are those who could justly condemn my advice, but I think that in some special cases the confession that is good for the soul should not be allowed to hurt innocent people. Maybe my faith needs to grow a bit. I do not want to provide excuses for not confessing, but I want, nevertheless, to send up some warning flags about confession.

Every great outpouring of the Holy Spirit on the Christian community has been marked with public confessions of sin. The great renewal movements at Asbury College and at Wheaton College are evidences of what I am talking about. In each of these cases special infillings of the Spirit occurred when chapel services at these schools were turned into revival meetings marked by much prayer and much confession of sin. The healthy part of both of these revivals was that the confessions were nonspecific. Persons admitted to sexual wrongdoings and other sins without going into detail. Students told of ill feelings that they had toward others without specifying their names. Consequently, the confessions did not reek of the sensationalism that can so easily mark such gatherings.

I have no desire to hear exhibitionists tell lurid tales that rival pornography. True spiritual confession elicits prayer, not longings for more of the dirty details. All of this is to say that confession is necessary, but all things are to be done decently and in order. Care and discretion are also Christian virtues.

Growing into Spiritual Maturity

One constantly asked question by those who seek to be filled with the Spirit is whether the "filling" is a sudden experience or a process that goes on over an extended period of time. William James, the famous Harvard psychologist, wrote about such spiritual dynamics from the perspective of a detached scientific observer. His claim was:

> To be converted, to be regenerated, to receive grace, to experience religion, to gain an assurance, are so many phrases which denote the process, gradual or sudden, by which a self hitherto divided, and consciously wrong inferior and unhappy, becomes unified and consciously right superior and happy, in consequence of its firmer hold upon religious realities. This at least is what conversion signifies in general terms, whether or not we believe that a direct divine operation is needed to bring such a moral change about.

From James' point of view there is no generalized pattern to be observed. He simply says that different people come into that spiritual ecstasy that rescues them from doubt and defeat in different ways. I want to add to James' insight that even those who feel themselves jolted into an enlivening new relationship with God should not delude themselves into believing that they have somehow achieved some kind of "complete" spiritual state. Spiritual maturity does not come that easy. There is no instant fix for the human condition, even for those whose Dionysian personalities predispose them to sudden flights of religious euphoria.

It certainly is a trip worth taking if you should find yourself caught up in the Spirit. Being transported into that joyful state of mind that makes everything in the world bright and wonderful is an experience not to be shunned. But such trips never prove to be shortcuts to that maturity in which we become complete in all that the Spirit can do for us. Coming to enjoy every spiritual benefit that is promised us in Romans 8 takes a lifetime of growing.

When Paul writes to the church at Philippi, he tries to deal with those perfectionists who claim instantaneous sanctification through some kind of special spiritual encounter. His words describing his own growing process are important because they are the testimony of a man who had enjoyed ecstasies that would make even some of the most sensational mystical experiences seem tame by comparison. Paul writes:

> That I may know him, and the power of his resurrection, and the fellowship of his sufferings, being made conformable unto his death; if by any means I might attain unto the resurrection of the dead. Not as though I had already attained, either were already perfect: but I follow after, if that I may apprehend that for which also I am apprehended of Christ Jesus. Brethren, I count not myself to have apprehended: but this one thing I do, forgetting those things which are behind, and reaching forth unto those things which are before, I press toward the mark for the prize of the high calling of God in Christ Jesus.
>
> *Philippians 3:10–14*

The words of Paul are a clear indication that reaching the fullness of all that God wants for us is a process. Becoming spiritual does not happen all at once. There are no shortcuts or instant solutions in the things of the Spirit. Only those who stick with it and endure until the end of the process will know what salvation is all about. "And ye shall be hated of all men for my name's sake: but he that shall endure unto the end, the same shall be saved" (Mark 13:13).

Chapter 7

Special Strokes
for Special Folks

P reaching has always proved to be a mysterious art form for me. It is more than just a privilege to share the gospel, because in preaching I am often aware of being *possessed* by the Holy Spirit. I am never quite sure when, and if, this possession is going to occur, but when it does, I know it. There are times in the middle of a sermon when I sense that what I am saying is no longer coming from me. I feel a power in my words and sense a flow of insights and truths that I never planned to express. There are times when I am preaching that I wish I could stand back and listen to myself, because I am so conscious that what I am saying has a quality and power that is beyond my own. In such times there is a coherence to my words and a sense that these words have been chosen carefully by Another.

The People As a Conduit for the Spirit

The essential condition that brings about this "possession" by the Spirit while I am preaching is what comes to me from the congregation. The congregation is the primary agent for bringing the Spirit to bear. There are times when a congregation is completely passive as I preach or, for lack of a kinder word, dead. When that is the case, I feel as if I am preaching *at* them. Preaching *at* a congregation is strenuous work, and on such occasions when I am finished, I am exhausted. However, there are times when the congregation becomes an active agent in creating the sermon. There are situations in which I feel something coming through the people to me. To put it in theological terms, I feel that the congregation has become sacramental and, thus, a means of grace. I get the sense that something is emerging between us that is more than and transcendent to anything we collectively possess.

When *real* preaching occurs, even the congregation becomes aware that we are experiencing the grace of God in a special way. Something mystical is happening in which we know that an unseen presence has taken hold and an awesome power has been released.

Rudolf Otto, the famous expert on religious phenomena, called what I am trying to describe the "mysterium tremendum." For the rest of us a simple acknowledgment that the Holy Spirit has come upon us is sufficient to express what we feel.

A testimony of the kind of spiritual interaction that can occur between preacher and congregation can be had by talking to almost any of us who have had the privilege to preach in an African-American church. This experience, in the finest sense, is a spiritual "trip." When a black congregation starts to "feed" the preacher with enthusiastic responses to the message, the preacher cannot help but be receptive. The black congregation often picks up a preacher and infuses him or her with a dynamism that changes not only the manner in which the sermon is delivered, but also its content.

African-American preachers often describe these times of unusual spiritual infilling and dynamism as occasions when they have "gotten down." I will not seek to explain what that expression means except to quote what I saw on a T-shirt worn by an African-American teenager: "It's a black thing and you wouldn't understand!"

Whenever I finish a sermon in which the Spirit has been actively creative, I am anything but exhausted. On the contrary, I am filled with energy. I am on a high. I feel as if I could do it again a hundred times and not be tired. The other thing that I feel is an intense and strange desire to be alone. I do not want to talk to anyone. I hate it when I have to shake hands with people and make small talk after the service. I sense that something miraculous has just occurred, and I do not want it to be disrupted with the trivial. I feel as if I had just been transported to the Mount of Transfiguration, and I would like to stay there a little longer before I have to come down.

When the "possession" happens, I know exactly what is going to follow. There are going to be many decisions for Christ. If I give an invitation for persons to raise their hands or to come down the aisle to demonstrate their commitment, the response will be immediate and usually in significant numbers.

On the other hand, I always get a bit upset when those who ask me to preach *insist* that I give an invitation at the end of the message. They *assume* that the Holy Spirit will work His miracles and that there will be decisions. I am never sure whether the awesome presence of the One who converts is going to be experienced. There is an impracticability to it. In the words of scripture:

> The wind bloweth where it listeth, and thou hearest the sound thereof, but canst not tell whence it cometh, and whither it goeth: so is every one that is born of the Spirit.
> *John 3:8*

Nothing is more pathetic than an evangelist who tries to make something happen when the Spirit has not "moved." Most of us have been at evangelistic meetings where the preacher gets the congregation to sing verse after verse of "Just As I Am" while he pleads for somebody . . . anybody to come forward. All of the tricks of the trade are employed by the desperate man as he tries to manipulate people out of their seats. As the invitation drags on, he usually waters down what is expected of respondents until just about anybody who has any desire at all to be a better kind of a person feels called upon to go down the aisle. I often feel so sorry for these suffering evangelists that I feel like going down the aisle myself just to help the poor man save a little face.

All of the "tricks" or attempts to manipulate become completely unnecessary and would be considered blasphemous when the dynamism of the Holy Spirit is moving. Responses are spontaneous and expected. There is an expectancy in the air and good things are happening. When the Spirit is in charge, there is no need to "lean on the flesh." In true evangelism the preacher senses the Spirit's moving among the people as much as he feels that he himself is possessed by the Spirit. That special concurrence makes any manipulative techniques offensive and unnecessary.

The best example of what I am trying to communicate can be found in the preaching of Billy Graham. Those who go over the content of Graham's sermons will find that they are filled with good solid evangelical theology, but they are hardly laced with brilliant new insights. His use of language is more than outstanding, but there are thousands of others who speak as well. His stature, appearance, and gestures all combine to facilitate an excellent presentation of his message. Yet all of those who study Graham's evangelistic crusades become immediately aware that something unexpected and especially dynamic takes place when he speaks. He *always* seems to have "it." People are affected in ways that are difficult to explain, but at just about every one of his crusades the meeting is filled with the expectancy that something special will happen. Some who only come out of idle curiosity find themselves caught up in a spiritual presence and power that moves them to go down the aisle to accept Christ as personal Savior and Lord. Many who come believing that they are already

Christians fall under the conviction of the Holy Spirit and, unexpectedly, find themselves responding to the invitation.

Over and over again interviews with those who responded to Graham's preaching and who have committed their lives to Christ will reveal that they cannot figure out just what it was that led them to make their decisions. Their descriptions of what happened go something like this:

> I don't understand why I made my decision. It was not any particular thing he said. As a matter of fact, I remember almost nothing of what he said. But while he was preaching, I felt as if God was speaking to me. When Billy gave the invitation to come forward, I was transported out of my seat and down the aisle.

I have no problem calling Billy Graham the greatest evangelist of the twentieth century. Nor do I need to be convinced that we will not see the likes of him again for a long, long time. The Holy Spirit is powerfully active when he preaches, and when he gives invitations, life-changing decisions are made on a scale that defies imagination.

Those of us who identify with Billy Graham's ministry credit the Holy Spirit for what is accomplished. We see what happens as mystical and miraculous.

The Spirit Overtakes Us When We Are Witnessing

Even if you can accept my strained efforts to explain the dynamism of the Holy Spirit that is often experienced in the context of preaching, you are probably saying to yourself, "I am no Billy Graham." You might even add, "I am not even a preacher."

The good news is that being an "up-front" communicator of the gospel is only one role in which the sense of being possessed by the Spirit can occur. It can also be experienced in the kind of everyday witnessing for Christ that can be a part of any committed

Christian's normative life. In those face-to-face encounters with people when the opportunity arises to share the message of salvation or to counsel a person with problems, a sense of being taken over and guided by the Spirit in what you say can happen.

In the Gospel of Matthew Jesus tells His disciples that as they go forth to witness they will experience persecution and will have to answer to many powerful and highly placed persons. He tells them:

> But when they deliver you up, take no thought how or what ye shall speak: for it shall be given you in that same hour what ye shall speak. For it is not ye that speak, but the Spirit of your Father which speaketh in you.
>
> *Matthew 10:19–20*

I believe that what Jesus said to his disciples back there for the situation they had to face is also applicable to us when we find ourselves in situations that require some counsel or a word of testimony. I am convinced that those who speak for Jesus in personal conversations can, much to their surprise, find themselves possessed by the Spirit. In such cases they will discover in what they are saying that they are going beyond their own knowledge and wisdom. When being possessed by the Spirit in the context of witnessing, Christians often find that they are miraculously capable of expressing profound truth with a brilliant clarity and simplicity.

A woman in my sociology class came to my office one day asking me *how* to talk to her boss about giving his life over to Christ. He was married and had children, but he was becoming sexually involved with one of the secretaries in the office. It was only a matter of time before several lives would be shattered. The woman felt that she could not stand by and let these people, for whom she cared so much, destroy themselves. She was not sure that she knew just what to say or how to go about approaching them on this painful subject. She wanted me to prescribe exactly how she should handle the situation.

I explained to her that I had no simple solution to her problem. I did not know these people and, therefore, lacked even the basic knowledge essential for a workable strategy. "However," I told her, "if you prayerfully prepare yourself and then just do it, you will be amazed at how well you will do."

The following week she came to my office again, bubbling with excitement. She explained how she had asked to see both of her friends privately in her boss's office. She told me how she had confronted them with what they were doing and asked them to ask Jesus to save them.

"It was amazing," she reported. "At first I was trembling like a leaf. As soon as I got going, the Lord took over. Just like you said, I had what were just the right words for them. I know that what I said was from the Lord," she continued, "because I never could have put together the words I said. I seemed to come up with exactly the things they needed to hear, and I found myself saying them in a manner that was both strong and gentle. I went into the office with no confidence in myself, but it did not make any difference. It was like the Lord put words in my mouth."

I was not surprised when she told me that both her boss and the secretary wept and repented. Both of them in that office surrendered their lives to the Lord.

Such stories are of great encouragement to any of us who are wondering if we have what it takes to speak a word for Christ. We need to know that if we try, it is possible for the Holy Spirit to direct us.

I head up an urban missionary program that calls upon young people who have very little experience to share the gospel with children and adults who live in low-cost housing projects in Philadelphia. These Christian workers are almost always surprised when they first try to witness, because they are more effective in sharing the gospel than they had ever expected to be. They usually testify to the fact that as they fearfully witnessed, they found themselves mysteriously empowered by the Spirit. Furthermore, they claim that they never would have gotten those responses if they had not been "possessed" by God.

The presence of the Holy Spirit in the context of personal witnessing or in providing spiritual counsel is especially wonderful when you become aware that the Spirit has prepared the other person for your message. You will soon learn that, before you arrive on the scene or say a word, the Spirit has preceded you and has softened the heart of the other person, and it is a real delight. It is this prior preparation that is the condition for your effectiveness. What is accomplished in such personal encounters is not to be attributed to your cleverness with words, but to the Spirit.

The Spirit in Koinonia

There is one context above all others wherein the Holy Spirit becomes *real* to those who seek His blessings. It is in and through the experience of *koinonia*. If that term is unfamiliar to you, allow me to define it simply as that special kind of Christian fellowship that those who are "in Christ" experience when they come together to minister to each other and to build up one another.

In the early days of Christianity such gatherings were the most notable features of the life of the church. They were more than enjoyable get-togethers in which Christians who had come to love one another could experience each other's presence. There was another dimension to the fellowship that they shared. In those times when they were together, Christians prayed and talked until there was a unity of consciousness. Their interaction produced an intense camaraderie. Something miraculous happened in those gatherings. When they were together and of one accord, says the scriptures, they experienced the Holy Spirit (Acts 2:46). This proved to be the most normative way in which the early church experienced the fullness of the Holy Spirit.

106

Christians, unlike those who come from other religions like Buddhism, Confucianism, and Hinduism, do not seek God in isolation from others while personally meditating in temples. Instead, they seek and experience God in togetherness. That is why Jesus told His disciples, "Where two or three are gathered together in my name, there am I in the midst of them" (Matt. 18:20). In that simple statement Jesus gives some hint of the communal nature of His family of faith.

Herman Schmalenbach, a prominent European sociologist, noted that those in the early Christian gatherings probably had something mystical happen to them. He contended that they experienced a "shared ecstasy." Instead of mystical experiences being private affairs, Schmalenbach observed that, with Christians, the ecstasy of the Spirit is something that is more likely to be enjoyed when they are in this special kind of fellowship that was ordered by Christ.

The Day of Pentecost

The first time that the early church was impacted by the Holy Spirit was when it followed the instructions of Jesus and stayed together, fasting and praying. Jesus, following His resurrection, had told His disciples to stay together and wait for the outpouring of the Spirit (Acts 1:14).

Forty days later, they were still together praying. It was then that the Spirit came upon them and the Christian movement was born:

> And when the day of Pentecost was fully come, they were all with one accord in one place. And suddenly there came a sound from heaven as of a rushing mighty wind, and it filled all the house where they were sitting. And there appeared unto them cloven tongues like as of fire, and it sat upon each of them. And they were all filled with the Holy Ghost, and began to speak with other tongues, as the Spirit gave them utterance.
>
> *Acts 2:1–4*

Over and over again the people of the early church were recharged by coming together like this and receiving the Holy Spirit from each other. They had come to learn that the Holy Spirit is communicated to God's people *through* their knowing the importance of gatherings. They were careful not to neglect "the assembling of [them]selves together" (Heb. 10:25).

When decisions had to be made or controversies had to be settled, they got together to experience the Spirit. It was when the Spirit had generated a consensus among them that they knew the will of God. When they needed confession and restoration because of sin among them, they found it through the Spirit in *koinonia*.

> Brethren, if a man be overtaken in a fault, ye which are spiritual, restore such an one in the spirit of meekness; considering thyself, lest thou also be tempted. Bear ye one another's burdens, and so fulfil the law of Christ. For if a man think himself to be something, when he is nothing, he deceiveth himself.
>
> *Galatians 6:1–3*

When they needed wisdom, teaching, and insight, they discovered that it was in *koinonia* that the Spirit raised up persons with the gifts to deliver these benefits.

When they needed healings, both physical and psychological, they found that it was through the Spirit's work in *koinonia* that their needs were met. Above all other means, the early Christians knew that *koinonia* was the instrument through which the Holy Spirit became known, and it was in *koinonia* that the work of the Holy Spirit was experienced.

Unfortunately, *koinonia* is not a common experience for contemporary Christians. In our modern world the church has become a lot of things, but it seldom offers its people the kind of fellowship that marked the life of Christians in the first century. That, of course, is precisely why mature spirituality is so rare among us. Without *koinonia*, the primary means for Christians to experience the dynamism of the Spirit, reports of what the Holy Spirit is doing among us are not as frequent as they should be.

Hope Through the Small Group Movement

The good news is that all across the country and around the world the need for *koinonia* is being recognized, and Christians everywhere are eagerly seeking ways to find it. The most common result of these quests is the emergence of what is called the Small Group movement. Seminaries are teaching their students a theology of *koinonia* and are training them to foster small group ministries in the churches that they will eventually serve. The new super churches that are now a major part of American Christianity have, in most instances, made organizing their members into small units that meet regularly a primary goal of their programming.

Those who are in youth ministry are increasingly getting teenagers into support groups. They realize that the spiritual strength which comes from small groups plays a primary role in enabling youth to overcome temptation.

Pastors have learned that those in small group ministries do not disdain traditional worship. They find a power and an aliveness in small groups that they bring to Sunday worship. What happens in small groups usually infuses churches with new vitality. It is as though people throughout Christendom suddenly have become aware that in small support groups they can encounter that spiritual presence that meets the hungers of their souls.

I personally can testify to the efficacy of small groups. My life has been changed significantly because of what has happened to me through participation in a group with three other men. We have met together weekly over the past several years. We have come to know each other, trust each other, and prayerfully carry each other's burdens. We have come to realize the power of the Holy Spirit in a special and wonderful way.

As an evangelist who regularly must counsel those who respond to the gospel, I make promoting small groups a dominant part of my ministry. When those who come down the aisle want to know what their next step should be, I always tell them that they should seek out two or three other Christians and form a support group that will meet at least once a week. I tell them to look for fellow Christians to whom they can relate comfortably. Those in the group should hold each other accountable as to how their Christian lives are being lived. The members should encourage and pray for one another. They should be available to meet one another's needs. I contend that, without the spiritual empowerment that can be derived from these small groups, any attempt to be a follower of Christ will end in failure and disillusionment.

It is important to recognize that Jesus Himself belonged to such a support group, and He regularly found in it the spiritual revitalization He needed to carry on His mission. It was with Peter, James, and John that He shared the mystical transcendence called the Transfiguration. It was with this close inner circle of disciples that He regularly went to solitary places to pray. And, when the time of His betrayal was at hand, it was with them that He retreated to Gethsemane to become spiritually prepared for the ordeal of crucifixion.

Jesus was not only very God of very God, as the creed says, He was also a man. As a man He sought empowerment through a small group. There can be no better example of how we all are to come into all that the Spirit can do for us.

Some Soft Suggestions on How to Make a Support Group Work

Very often those who start small groups at my urging come back to me and tell me that they need help in figuring out how to make their groups live up to their promise. They want to have a guide scheme like "Ten Steps to a Successful Small Group Experience." In my replies I am reluctant to spell out too much of how their meetings should be structured. I believe that it is dangerous for anyone to prescribe just how to make *koinonia* happen. I do not think that there is a single formula as to how to ensure a meaningful and spiritually enlivening group. But what I am able to do on these occasions is to describe what our support group does and what spiritual disciplines we have incorporated into our times together.

In our particular group we have made a conscious decision *not* to make our weekly get-together into a Bible study. We all realize the need for Bible study and the need to exegete scripture. But Bible study is something that each of us can do on his own. We do not want to make our times together primarily intellectual. Instead, we read the scripture out loud to one another and then reflect on what we sense God is saying to us through His word right then and there. We let the scriptures serve as a stimulus for reflection on what is going on in our respective lives. We tell one another what the scripture we have just read got us to think about. Often our discussions range far and wide from the subject matter of the biblical passage with which we started. The Bible gives us a place to start. However, we soon are analyzing personal needs and problems. We always try to help each other to find ways to better live out the gospel in our respective lives.

The second thing we do is pray. Of course, there are the usual concerns that fathers and husbands have. But there is one other thing we do that might prove useful to those who want some direction in plotting small group get-togethers. We pray our way through the Psalms. This is a spiritual discipline that is regularly carried out by Benedictine monks. We find the practice very meaningful within our gatherings.

I believe that the Psalms were meant to be prayed. I see them as the outpouring of the devotional giants of centuries past. In them, David and the other psalm writers were giving vent to their deepest feelings about God, the world, and the people who were part of their everyday lives. As such they provided incredible vehicles for putting into words emotions and yearnings that we find hard to otherwise articulate. As we pray the Psalms, I often have a sense that the same Holy Spirit that inspired them is inspiring us and is giving significance and power to the words that are obviously from the Father.

The weekly get-togethers of our small group are not much more than that. But do not underestimate what goes on in them just because of the simplicity of the format. The Spirit can be profound in the midst of such simplicity.

Every group must establish its own style. Do not be afraid to try new ways of seeking the Spirit if the first ways that you try fail. Most of all, be patient! It takes a lot of time to become *koinonia*. Only those who are willing to wait can expect the miracle.

Chapter 8

Picking Out the Phonies

There are a lot of phonies in the Pentecostal movement. That should come as no surprise. From the very beginning of the life of the church there have been those who have either feigned having spiritual powers or who have sought to gain spiritual powers for their own profit. Perhaps the most famous instance of a religious charlatan can be found in the biblical account of Simon the sorcerer:

> But there was a certain man, called Simon, which beforetime in the same city used sorcery, and bewitched the people of Samaria, giving out that himself was some great one: to whom they all gave heed, from the least to the greatest, saying, This man is the great power of God. And to him they had regard, because that of long time he had bewitched them with sorceries. But when they believed Philip preaching the things concerning the kingdom of God, and the name of Jesus Christ, they were baptized, both men and women. Then Simon himself believed also: and when he was baptized, he continued with Philip, and wondered, beholding the miracles and signs which were done. Now when the apostles which

were at Jerusalem heard that Samaria had received the word of God, they sent unto them Peter and John: who, when they were come down, prayed for them, that they might receive the Holy Ghost: (For as yet he was fallen upon none of them: only they were baptized in the name of the Lord Jesus.) Then laid they their hands on them, and they received the Holy Ghost. And when Simon saw that through laying on of the apostles' hands the Holy Ghost was given, he offered them money, saying, Give me also this power, that on whomsoever I lay hands, he may receive the Holy Ghost. But Peter said unto him, Thy money perish with thee, because thou hast thought that the gift of God may be purchased with money. Thou hast neither part nor lot in this matter: for thy heart is not right in the sight of God. Repent therefore of this thy wickedness, and pray God, if perhaps the thought of thine heart may be forgiven thee. For I perceive that thou art in the gall of bitterness, and in the bond of iniquity. Then answered Simon, and said, Pray ye to the Lord for me, that none of these things which ye have spoken come upon me. And they, when they had testified and preached the word of the Lord, returned to Jerusalem, and preached the gospel in many villages of the Samaritans.

Acts 8:9–25

Jesus himself warned these disciples in Matthew 24:24 that there would be false prophets who would lead many astray with their displays of "signs and wonders."

For there shall arise false Christs, and false prophets, and shall show great signs and wonders; insomuch that, if it were possible, they shall deceive the very elect.

Furthermore, Jesus let it be known that there would be spiritual pretenders who not only would deceive others, but also themselves. In other words, Jesus told us that there would be "sincere" phonies who would not realize their own self-deception until the day of judgment.

> Not every one that saith unto me, Lord, Lord, shall enter into the kingdom of heaven; but he that doeth the will of my Father which is in heaven. Many will say to me in that day, Lord, Lord, have we not prophesied in thy name? and in thy name have cast out devils? and in thy name done many wonderful works? And then will I profess unto them, I never knew you: depart from me, ye that work iniquity.
> *Matthew 7:21–23*

Sometimes these phonies are easy to spot. But at other times we say very little in the way of condemnation, even though we have an uneasy feeling about them. We look at this latter type and have nothing we can put our fingers on, but, justified or unjustified, we are left with our suspicions.

We should always be ready to err on the side of believing too much. We should be careful when we judge. We should be reluctant to call people phonies lest we make serious mistakes and miss out on what God is trying to do in our midst. On the other hand, the scriptures do call us to a ministry of spiritual discernment. What that means is that it is every Christian's responsibility to figure out whether or not those who come to exercise spiritual gifts among us are for real. "Beloved, believe not every spirit, but try the spirits whether they are of God: because many false prophets are gone out into the world" (1 John 4:1).

The Real Jerks

Sometimes there is something ludicrous about the pretenses. For instance, a friend of mine was at a healing service of one of the more flamboyant Pentecostal evangelists on the circuit. This healer/evangelist claimed to have a direct line to God. He claimed to receive special messages from God that were to be delivered to members of the audience. In this particular case these special messages and the associated blessings would be given to anyone who demonstrated that he or she had the faith to believe. As might be well imagined, the necessary faith could be demonstrated only by a "faith gift" of money. Anyone who was willing to show his or her faith by handing over one hundred dollars to "the ministry" would be eligible for a special "word from the Lord" and a miracle that would meet a great need in a believer's life.

After having fleeced the crowd of several thousand dollars, this "man of God" closed his eyes and, with his facial muscles tensed and blood vessels protruding because of strain, he gave the impression that he was tuned into the cosmic mind of the Eternal. After several moments this phony let it be known that he was receiving a message from God.

With all the finesse of a con artist, he spoke in a deep and authoritative voice as though the Almighty One was speaking through him. "There is someone here with arthritis in her right elbow," he declared.

"Stand up! God has told me about you, and He has told me that He wants to heal you."

Nobody stood, much to my friend's delight.

Then this money-grubbing evangelist took another shot at getting his word from the Lord with an even more thunderous declaration, "Somebody here has arthritis in the right arm. Stand! God wants to heal you."

My friend assumed, as I am sure the "man of God" in the pulpit assumed, that out of a crowd of about twenty-five hundred people there had to be at least one person who had arthritis in the right arm. But still nobody stood.

The uneasiness of the crowd and the growing panic of the "man of God" became increasingly obvious, and my friend wondered what would happen next.

Then, meekly, the evangelist retreated from his former bold declaration and quietly said, "Well, maybe it's the left arm."

Unfortunately, my friend could not contain himself and broke out laughing. What was worse was that nobody else seemed to see any humor in all of this. Quickly, two tough-looking ushers appeared and beckoned him to follow them. He was not about to argue with these religious bouncers, so he followed them as they ushered him out of the tent meeting.

My friend did not see how anybody could swallow what this phony was handing out. It seemed to him that this so-called man of God was an obvious fraud. But my friend was wrong. Recently, this particular faith healer has begun to appear regularly on television. He is now carrying his financial scam to the millions across America who seem all too ready to be taken in by such antics.

So far as I am concerned, "charismatic" preachers like this one are easy to judge. The phoniness of what they do has a long history and, as indicated earlier, was evident from the earliest days of the church. These would-be miracle workers and prophets expose themselves for what they are by one simple fact. They tie up what they do with money. Whenever the religious leader makes money a condition for experiencing God's blessings, you can write him off. God never links money with grace. And God does not need a gift of a hundred dollar bill as a sign of your faith. God knows the heart of every person without any outward expressions.

What the Church Fathers Had to Say About Phonies

One of the oldest pieces of Christian writing is the *Didache*. This particular book of religious instruction was put together shortly after the time of the Apostles. It became part of the literature that church historians refer to as the writings of the Church Fathers. A reading of the *Didache* will reveal that religious rip-off artists like the "man of God" I just described were doing their thing way back then. The instruction of the church fathers concerning how to spot such phonies is as follows:

However, not everyone speaking in ecstasy is a prophet, except he has the ways of the Lord about him. So by their ways must the true and the false prophet be distinguished. No prophet who in an ecstasy orders the table spread, must partake of it; otherwise, he is a false prophet. Any prophet that teaches the truth yet does not live up to his teaching, is a false prophet. When a prophet, once approved as genuine, does something by way of symbolizing the Church in an earthly manner, yet does not instruct others to do all that he himself is doing, he is not liable to your judgment, for his judgment rests with God. After all, the Prophets of old acted in the same manner. But if anyone says in ecstasy, "Give me money," or something else, you must not listen to him. However, should he tell you to give something for others who are in need, let no one condemn him.

Didache 11:8–12

Such warnings did not keep the church itself from becoming involved with these practices. By the time of the Protestant Reformation in the fifteenth century, the sale of the blessings of God for a suitable price had become commonplace. In reality it was the sale of indulgences (i.e., payment to escape the pain of purgatory) that was the primary evil abroad in the church that moved Martin Luther to start the revolt that has divided Christendom for centuries.

The grace of God is not for sale primarily because it is grace. God gives what He gives out of love, and it is His love that keeps Him from withholding any good gift that he can give to us (Ps. 84:11).

Thus the first mark of a phony charismatic who claims to have Pentecostal gifts is that he or she connects ministry to others with special offerings or "faith promise gifts." The dollar sign is not a sign that brings on the work of the Spirit. Christians should give, but they should give in love—not to get some special blessing—and woe unto those who do the selling.

The Scriptural Test

The second consideration that should be given to those who are exercising charismatic gifts is whether what is being propagated is in harmony with scripture. I know of one pastor of an independent Pentecostal congregation who claimed that he had received a word from the Lord to divorce his wife and marry another woman in the church. It seems obvious to me that the man was not to be believed. The Spirit does not lead us in ways that contradict the teachings of the Bible.

It is clear that the scriptures become the ultimate check and balance on claims that are made by charismatic preachers and miracle workers about their ministries. In the Book of Acts we have the laudatory words about the Berean church whose members checked out every would-be prophet who came to town by figuring out whether his message and actions harmonized with scripture (Acts 17:11).

Wild as it may seem, the pastor who told his congregation that God had told him to divorce his wife and marry another woman got away with it. The congregation bought his "word from the Lord." They should have realized that the Holy Spirit does not lead contrary to what the Bible teaches. But they didn't! This is just one more example of how a movement, which I believe is of God, can be twisted and abused to serve sinful human interests.

Recently there has been a branch of the Charismatic movement that has come up with a relatively new brand of charismatic healing. These new preachers on the block of neopentecostals claim that a demon must be cast out in order to heal a person's illness or disability. There is the suggestion that demons are responsible for all physical maladies. Furthermore, they claim that only by naming the demon can deliverance be gained.

Of course those who are leaders of this movement claim to have received revelations from God giving them the names of the demons, can discern which one possesses a given victim, and thus are able to exercise power over the demon by ordering it by name.

I have been amazed at the spreading influence of these particular charismatic healers. People have flocked to them. Their popularity has spread not only across America but throughout Europe, New Zealand, and Australia. I must admit that I am very threatened by these men because so many people that I know and respect have bought into their movement.

Yet I keep on asking for the biblical basis for their teachings. Where do these men get off talking about the names of particular demons when the Bible makes no mention of them? And how can they claim that knowing these names is essential to casting them out when the Bible does not suggest such a formula for healing?

A deep concern of mine is that, according to this new version of the Charismatic movement, every person who is crippled or blind or physically handicapped in some other way is suffering because of a demon. That ticks me off! It is tough enough for these hurting people to live with these infirmities without some would-be prophets laying a demon-possession trip on them.

I asked one of the spokesmen of this movement to explain the condition of a former student of mine who was painfully crippled in spite of the fact that he was one of the most mature Christians I knew. The explanation I received was that it was undoubtedly the sin of one of his parents, grandparents, or great grandparents that was responsible. According to this particular charismatic leader, the sin of one of his ancestors allowed a demon to enter the family lineage, and the demon was passed on generation to generation and was now doing its work in my crippled friend. And yes, if the demon could be named, he could be cast out by a man of faith. That kind of theology is so detached from the Bible that I have to reject it.

Sola scriptura (meaning "scripture alone") was the motto of the Protestant Reformation. Martin Luther used it, and he contended that on religious matters he had to be persuaded either by scripture or by conscience. I like Luther's approach to things, and I have a pretty good idea as to what he and the other Reformers would have to say to this new breed of Charismatics and their new methodology of curing human maladies. They all held the Bible as the final authority for faith and life.

The Traditions That Cannot Be Ignored

Among those who have been in the church and who have spoken for the church over the centuries have been a host of saintly people. None of the likes of Saint Francis, Thomas à Kempis, Saint Teresa, John Wesley, Dwight L. Moody, Meister Eckhart, Count Zinzendorf, William Penn, Saint Ignatius, Fanny Crosby, Henrietta Miers, and our contemporary Mother Teresa were perfect. But nevertheless, they represent a holy tradition. It is this tradition that cannot be ignored.

There are some common threads that run through what these saints said and did. There is a spiritual heritage that they have generated which must be taken seriously. When all of a sudden some Charismatic-come-lately has a new revelation that stands in opposition to what these saints of the church have shared with us for centuries, we ought to be more than a little suspicious about the veracity of the "new" revelation. It seems very unlikely that all of those deeply committed saints of the past had an inadequate faith. I find it hard to believe that it has remained for modern-day voices in the Charismatic movement to reveal some new deep truths that God failed to make known to the great saints of yesteryear.

The scripture has been interpreted by godly people for almost two thousand years. Among them there has been a good consensus as to how they should be interpreted. That consensus is what the theologians and Bible scholars call the tradition of the church. I do not claim that this tradition is infallible. It should by no means be considered to be on the same level as the authority of scripture itself. It is not set in stone, nor should it be equated with the Word of God. Nevertheless, it cannot be discounted as a basis against which new religious teaching and practices should be measured.

When someone claims to have some special spiritual gift that provides some brand new insights to what God is about, and those insights stand against the historic traditions of the church, we ought to seriously question what we are being told.

So far as I am concerned some of the most healthy and wholesome expressions of the Charismatic movement can be found in the Roman Catholic and Anglican (Episcopalian) churches. Those charismatics who live out their faith within the context of these particular churches have been nurtured on a healthy respect for the historic traditions of Christianity. With this criterion they are able to keep the sensationalist tendencies of the Charismatic movement under control. They have a sense that what is happening now must somehow fit with what has gone before. As they try to figure out what to accept and what to reject in any new movement of the Spirit they readily admit to having to be responsible to those who have gone before them.

> Wherefore seeing we also are compassed about with so great a cloud of witnesses, let us lay aside every weight, and the sin which doth so easily beset us, and let us run with patience the race that is set before us.
>
> *Hebrews 12:1*

The sense of faithfulness to tradition among those in the Anglican and Roman Catholic denominations has given them a defense against those phonies and those heresies that deviate from what God has entrusted to the faithful of the church down through the ages.

As a case in point, allow me to remind you once again of those who claim that in order to cast out demons the exorcist must know the name of the demons. These new charismatics, as you may recall, claim that those without the actual names of demons can have no power over them. My problem with this kind of teaching is that there is just about no historic precedent for it in the history of Christendom. Stories about casting out demons are as old as the early church and as recent as the case studies of the psychotherapist M. Scott Peck. Yet the need to know the names of the demons in order to destroy their power is not mentioned in any significant way during the long account of Christian ministry. This realization makes me more than a little suspicious as to the validity of the new doctrine.

The Need for Confrontation

When deviance from what is biblical and what has been part of the nominal life of Christians down through history becomes evident, it is the obligation of Christians to call a halt to things. Generally that means confronting those who are responsible for the strange new ways of doing things with your doubts.

Jay Kesler, the president of Taylor University, once told me about being part of a missionary conference wherein one of the speakers had an array of spectacular stories about what he claimed God was doing in India. Among them were stories about bringing dead people back to life. According to this particular speaker, this was happening regularly as part of the ongoing evangelistic ministry of missions.

Jay related to me how he sensed that what was being said was devoid of authenticity, seemed out of line from what historically was experienced in the normal life of the church, and appeared to be designed primarily to give the speaker a position of awesome prestige. Jay did not let the speaker get away with what he perceived to be phoniness. So he privately confronted the man and told him that he suspected that what was being preached was bogus.

The man admitted that his stories were false, but he claimed that he meant no harm. The stories about raising people from the dead were told, so he said, to encourage the church and to give Christians more confidence. I fail to see the logic of such an argument. It does not seem to me that the church will be helped by such stories. Instead I think the reverse would be true. If the stories are believed, we cannot help but ask why that kind of power does not thrive in the churches of which we are a part. Stories like these only foster a sense of unnecessary inferiority among a lot of saints.

I suppose that if the man had denied the accusations, the next thing to do would be to follow the steps outlined in Matthew 17. Jay would have confronted the man a second time, but on the second occasion he would bring a witness with him. According to the directions given by Jesus Himself, if there is still no confession and repentance, then the matter ought to be brought before the elders. And if that does not work, then the church congregation to which the offending person belongs ought to be called upon to judge these matters.

Unfortunately, a number of Charismatic leaders on the contemporary American scene do not have congregations that will hold them accountable for what they say and do. That, of course, is one of the great flaws of the movement. Too often, a Charismatic preacher starts his own congregation from scratch, and he rules that congregation with almost absolute power. Such congregations are usually independent of any denominational affiliation so that for all intents and purposes the preacher ends up as a kind of lone ranger.

Be careful when you come across charismatic leaders like this. We all need accountability structures to keep us honest, and when a Christian leader finds that he does not have to answer to anyone for his actions, he has set himself up for trouble. Once again, it is no surprise to me that some of the healthiest expressions of charismatic leadership are in the Anglican and Roman Catholic churches. Those who exercise the gifts of the Spirit within these traditions are not on their own. They have to answer to an ecclesiastical hierarchy which, for all of its faults and problems, still keeps its people from going off the deep end. Phonies have to be stopped and it is a primary ministry of the church to stop them.

Spiritual Warfare

Chapter 9

Not Overdoing the Peretti Thing

F rank Peretti has written a couple of best-selling novels that have done us all a great favor. These books, *This Present Darkness* and *Piercing the Darkness*, have awakened millions of Christians to a consciousness that we are all engaged in spiritual warfare. For those who have been raised in one of the Eastern Orthodox churches these books might possibly have been less necessary. The Orthodox churches have always had a deep understanding that a great battle rages in heavenly places between the demonic followers of Satan and the angelic agents of our Lord. In the theologies of the Orthodox church, the primary dimension of the doctrine of salvation is focused on how Jesus on the cross broke the power of the demonic forces and initiated a triumph over darkness, which is now being lived out in the church and will be solidified in all of its glory when Christ returns. Between now and the Second Coming of Christ the demonic powers are still among us, and they are still raising havoc. According to the Eastern Orthodox theologies, we must fight against these evil powers. We are called to be a part of the great battle and join with Christ and His angels to the end that the agents of the Evil One are vanquished. This particular theme is picked up in Ephesians 6:12:

For we wrestle not against flesh and blood, but against principalities, against powers, against the rulers of the darkness
of this world, against spiritual wickedness in high places.

What Frank Peretti has done in his amazingly popular books
is to make this struggle against evil spirits understandable in everyday life. Peretti suggests that evil spirits prompt people to do
mean things to each other, to be selfish, to turn from spiritual
disciplines like prayer and Bible study, and to become disruptive
influences in their homes and churches. He convincingly proposes
that there are specific evil spirits assigned to each of us with the
task of turning you and me into agents of Satan's will. Accord-
ingly, those in Christian ministry are given the tasks of making us
aware of what is going on and helping us to defend ourselves
against this onslaught of demonic powers.

With Peretti the idea of Satan's directing demons to divert
Christians from the ways that lead to spiritual maturity is taken
way beyond that which what was suggested in C. S. Lewis' famous book *The Screwtape Letters*. With Peretti, spiritual warfare
for the Christian is seen as a personal struggle that each of us must
carry on against devils. In his writings this struggle is given a real-
ism and a specificity that is rare in modern Christian literature.
While Peretti's books are novels, what he is describing is not meant
to be understood as make-believe.

We dare not turn away from the description of spiritual warfare given by Peretti simply because it does not fit in with our
modern world-view. We have been socialized in our culture to look
at things in such a way as to preclude understanding any human behavior as being significantly influenced by demons. But, as any
anthropologist will tell us, that conclusion only reflects a cultural bias.
The way we have been socialized to view things is not necessarily the
way they really are. It is no great secret to social scientists that our
culturally biased understanding of what is real and what is not real
prevents us from apprehending a great deal of truth.

The Bible establishes a clear case for what Peretti claims. According to the scriptures, there are demons at work in our world. Satan, unlike God, cannot be everywhere watching over everyone. Thus, he has his agents of evil to be where he isn't in order to do what he wants.

If this is too much for you to swallow it is probably because you are too much controlled by the imbued perspectives on reality that go with living in our times. There is no empirical evidence that Peretti is right *or* wrong. The Bible says he's right, and if you disagree I contend it is probably because our culture has predisposed you to believe what you do. C. S. Lewis, the brilliant Oxford don, was able to break through culturally prescribed blinders to believe in demons, and he went on to warn all of us that a primary strategy of Satan is to get us to believe that Satan and his legions do not exist. Peretti would have us believe that struggles against demons are part of what the Christian life is all about.

Your Devil May Be Too Small

A primary problem that I have with the wave of awareness of devils generated by the Peretti phenomena is that what he describes and what people have come to believe in may be far too small. Certainly the demonic forces that we must confront in spiritual warfare are much more threatening than the little gremlins who hide behind doors or lurk in dark places waiting to get us. The evil ones who would destroy us are more than that in every way. They present themselves to us in attractive forms and through subtle means. They seduce us and remold us through systems and structures that may not at first seem at all threatening. They enslave us in ways that leave us unaware that we have become slaves, ways that prove so attractive that we actually want the slavery they create to confine us. They are forces that make us so comfortable with evil that we are confused into thinking that what they offer is good.

135

Getting back to that famous verse on spiritual warfare cited earlier, it is important that we add some depth to our understanding of what the apostle Paul is talking about when he writes in Ephesians 6:12 that we are wrestling "against principalities, against powers, against the rulers of the darkness of this world, against spiritual wickedness in high places."

A good aid in this task is found in Hendrik Berkhof's seminal work entitled *Christ and the Powers*. Every once in a while there is a book that provides crucial enlightenment on urgent concerns, and this little book fits into that category. Berkhof explores some of the more profound dimensions of what Paul means by his often-used phrase "principalities and powers."

In reading this short book you will learn that when Paul talks about principalities and powers he is referring to all those forces outside of us that influence and direct our behavior. He is referring not only to demons but to such social institutions as the government, the educational system, the economic system, and the family. Principalities and powers also refers to such things as the media and advertising. If Paul were among us today he would certainly consider television to be a major principality and power that impacts our lives. Who can question the ways in which such forces as MTV have molded the mind-set of a generation?

What Paul is telling us, according to Berkhof, is that these principalities and powers were originally created and ordained by God to contribute to our good and well-being (Col. 1:6). However, because of sin, we have not only given the Evil One a stronghold in our personal lives, but we have also allowed him to gain control over these principalities and powers as well. Government, television, and other principalities and powers are now, according to Berkhof's understanding of Paul, exercising horrendous negative influences on us. Those demonic forces which would hurt us work through these means to bring us into Satan's sphere of control.

Heading up a missionary program that is designed to minister to inner-city teenagers and children, I have become greatly aware of how one particular principality and power, the educational system, has become a destructive force in the lives of tens of thousands of youngsters. I believe that this principality and power was ordained by God to help young people into fruitful and worthwhile lives. But something has gone wrong. In some of the high schools of Philadelphia the educational process has left so many students alienated and demoralized that less than 30 percent of them graduate. Of those who do graduate more than 35 percent are functional illiterates.

These inner-city schools are now the breeding grounds for drug abuse and crime. A note written to the pastor of my church by students at a neighboring junior high school reads:

> Dear Dr. Campbell,
>   Pray for Sayre Junior High. Have your church pray for us. Things are very wrong here. People are fighting all the time. All the good teachers left in January. They just put in metal detectors to try to keep guns out of the school. We need help. . . .

There is a kind of demonic possession that is overtaking this school. Satan is imposing destructive influences, and he is destroying people's lives. This principality and power must be delivered. The demonic presence in the school must be challenged. Christians are needed to engage in spiritual warfare and reclaim this school for the kingdom of God.

Spiritual Warfare and Rock Music

Without describing how spiritual warfare plays itself out in all areas of everyday life, let us focus on two areas that deserve some special attention in contemporary culture. They are rock music and witchcraft.

Do not think for one minute that I am about to launch into one of those tirades against rock music and claim that it all comes straight from the devil. While I must contend that some rock music lyrics I have heard are so filled with descriptions of obscene sex and violence that they have to be declared as unfit for the entertainment of any reasonable Christian, it is not primarily the lyrics or the beat of rock music that is the focus of my attention. Instead I am concerned about what happens at rock concerts. I am fascinated at what emanates from the masses of young people who gather for these Dionysian extravaganzas.

Emile Durkheim, perhaps the most seminal thinker in the history of modern sociology, observed that in mass gatherings (such as rock concerts) there can arise what he called a "collective effervescence." According to Durkheim, those who are on stage are able to prompt interactive processes in a crowd so that a kind of collective emotion is generated within a short period of time. Once created, suggests Durkheim, this collective emotion seems to take on a life of its own.

The crowd in such situations is no longer simply a collection of individuals but comes to share in a kind of group consciousness that sweeps away individual states of awareness. Persons lose their sense of being separate and distinct from the crowd. They participate in a kind of wholistic group psychology. There is emotional content to this shared consciousness so that the participants feel things that transcend anything that they as individuals might experience.

Something emerges *sui generis* (as Durkheim would say) that is more than the total of all the emotions of those who make up the crowd. Something unique and overpowering has been created that imposes itself on each and every member of the crowd.

The individuals in such settings cease being who they were and take on the collective consciousness of the crowd. Persons are transported into a state of emotional and psychological awareness that transcends anything they have known in their in-dividualized condition.

Anyone who has ever studied the audience of a rock concert certainly knows what Durkheim is talking about. The young people at these explosive gatherings are transported beyond themselves and enter into a shared ecstasy. They seem possessed by a dynamic that comes from the group. They are no longer individuals. They are swallowed up, contends Durkheim, in a collective effervescence that is capable of altering their behavior.

It is important for me to emphasize that the shared collective consciousness at rock concerts can be either good or evil. We must not think that this force is necessarily evil just because it transcends individualism. Actually the collective effervescence can be very positive and can have a godly impact on those in the crowd. Certain rock musicians (like the band U2 or Bruce Springsteen) can elicit a collective consciousness that is filled with hope and faith. I have seen rock concerts that have generated a collective effervescence which had something of the fruits of the Spirit (Gal. 5:22–23) evident in it. Those who come away from these "good" concerts seem to take on a love, joy, and peace that comes from beyond themselves. What they share in the concerts seems to be holy and of God.

But I have also seen rock concerts generate a demonic presence; I have sensed something evil happening to the young people in these concerts. In those situations I get the feeling that these teenagers are being swept away by a presence that is dark and foreboding. It is as though those in the crowd are being caught up and captivated by something diabolical.

When the "evil" concert is over I do not expect that the young people will be the same. What I really feel is that they are being swallowed up in something that will destroy them. Sometimes I feel a demon of sadistic sex pervading the concert. Other times there is a spirit of defiant contempt toward God. I come away from these concerts convinced that something has happened that will be filled with defiance and impurities. I have to say that these kinds of concerts frighten me. There is something sinister about them.

Out of all this I suppose you can get some idea as to where I am coming from in my evaluation of rock music. I am not as high on analyzing what the musicians say about themselves as I am convinced that they must be judged by their fruits (Matt. 7:16). Rock musicians are the contemporary pied pipers and prophets. They are leading a vast army of young people, and we must be very careful as to where they are leading them and what is happening to them on the journey. The spirits that are conjured up by those electrifying performers must be tested to see if they are of God (1 John 4:1).

Many parents find that in trying to rescue their children from the spiritual destruction that has resulted from their immersion in a rock culture, they are not just struggling against flesh and blood, but they are wrestling with principalities and powers. They are finding that spiritual warfare is a lot more complicated than Peretti's books suggest.

Taking Witchcraft Seriously

Whenever people start talking about spiritual warfare there is always some discussion about witches' covens and ritualistic demonic ceremonies. Those of us who claim to be rational and to possess a modern perspective on reality have a tendency to discount this kind of talk and put it in the category of make-believe. That, I believe, may be a serious mistake.

On one occasion I was contacted by the principal of a high school in upstate New York who asked if I would come up to his school and talk to the staff and student body about witchcraft. I thought this was a strange request, but he went on to explain that several students were involved in a coven, and three of that group had recently committed suicide. He went on to explain that witchcraft had become a common part of student life at the school and that he was afraid of it all. This particular high school had to cancel its graduation exercises that year because several students had made a pact to commit suicide simultaneously during the ceremonies.

There are stories of ritualistic suicides and murders all across America. Suicide is now the second major cause of death among teenagers, and I am convinced that a significant proportion of them are related to witchcraft.

Those who are involved in working with young people can give story upon story of having to deal with witchcraft in their ministries. Usually those who get involved in such things do so out of a desire to be a part of something that is off beat and weirdly fascinating. Only too late do they discover that they have been ensnared by forces beyond their control. I talked with one fifteen-year-old who explained that going to the rituals of a coven was something she did just for fun. It was only after she got involved that she discovered that something real was going on.

If all of this seems off the wall and made-up, it may be because you are disconnected from today's youth culture. You may have lost touch with what they think and believe. And if you think that their talk about witchcraft and covens is all the stuff of imagination, it may only be because you do not take the testimonies of the participants seriously.

The Will to Power

I am anything but an expert on such matters, but I have talked to a good number of young people who have been involved with witchcraft, and I have tried to find out what the great attraction is. I have been curious as to why anybody would want to get involved with the devil. Did these young people think that the eventual consequences of their relations with the demonic would be anything other than disastrous?

141

What I discovered is that the young people were attracted to the demonic and to the religion of Satan primarily in a quest for *power*. "Power," explained one teenage boy, "is what this thing is all about." He went on to explain that he had always felt like "nothing" and that he could never do what he wanted or get what he wanted. There were girls he liked, he told me, but these girls never seemed to like him. There were guys at school that pushed him around, and there didn't seem to be anything he could do about it. His parents, he believed, never thought he could do anything right and were always putting him down.

With such feelings about his inability to control his destiny, to be what he wanted, and to get some respect from his peers, he was an easy target for enlistment in his high school coven. Those in his high school who were into witchcraft talked about the powers they had because of their alliance with the spirits of darkness. It was this promise of power that made him open to involvement with witchcraft. The pain of powerlessness and insignificance were too much for him to handle, and he became more than curious about the possibilities of overcoming these shortcomings through this new religion.

This young man told me that it seemed like a "lot of corny stuff" at first, but it seemed to work. He said that he felt like he had gained a certain magnetism. Girls were interested in him, and guys who used to threaten him seemed like they were afraid of him. He felt sure of himself for the first time in his life. He felt like he was in control and that nobody had better stand in his way. "I walked differently," he told me. "I could feel the difference. I had powers and I knew it."

When I asked him if he had thought about what all of his witchcraft activities would lead to in the end, he simply said, "I never thought about it at all. I was so much into what was happening to me that I put the future out of my mind."

The thing that got him out of witchcraft was what happened in one of the weekly rituals of his coven. As part of the ceremonies he and his friends would kill stray cats and dogs and wipe the blood of these animals on their faces and bodies. The horror of this never hit him until one day he realized that they were about to kill his own dog. The shock of seeing the animal he loved about to have its neck slashed shook him to the awareness of how evil all of this was. He rescued his dog, went home, and the next day went to a minister of a Pentecostal church and asked for help.

Perhaps stories like this are made up. But I hear too many like them to write them off. In a community near mine, Upper Merion Township, there was a sensational murder of a woman and her children. As the story unfolded, it was revealed that she was part of a coven. There was even a suggestion that the murder of her children was part of a demonic ceremony. The story made headlines and was even made into a television drama.

In California a mass murderer has declared that he is a worshiper of Satan. There are numerous stories that parallel his from a score of other sources.

You may want to write all of this off, but I must say that my skepticism about these matters has greatly diminished over the last few years. A look at the shelves of any sophisticated bookstore will reveal that books on the powers of darkness are now bestsellers. People do believe in these kinds of things, whether they are real or not. Personally, I think more is going on out there than we know. I believe that Satan is alive and well and living on Planet Earth. And while demons may not be hiding behind every rock waiting to get us, and while they may not be sitting on our shoulders whispering evil suggestions into our ears, something is going on out there, and we had better be ready to deal with it. All the dimensions of spiritual warfare would leave me a bit scared if it were not for the Holy Spirit. I know that He who is in me is greater than the Evil One who is out there in the world (1 John 4:4). In the battles that we must wage against the powers of darkness we need not assume only a defensive posture. God provides the wherewithal for us to attack evil and to drive it back. We need not be afraid or ashamed, for the good news is that we have the power of God at our disposal (Rom. 1:16).

A New Kind of Prayer

If we are to go on the attack against witchcraft and other forms of the demonic, then we must learn ways to use different kinds of prayers that for many of us might prove novel and strange. Most of us know how to pray *to* God. Indeed, for most Christians praying *to* God is all that we know how to do when it comes to prayer. However, there is another way to pray, and if we are to be effective Christian warriors, we must learn this other way. It is to allow ourselves to become the lens *through* whom God can focus His power on those who need deliverance.

It is one thing to call upon God to move on someone who is caught up in dark things. But is it quite another to allow ourselves to become channels *through* whom God directs His saving power toward those in spiritual danger. God can energize us with His Spirit and make us into what might be analogous to laser weapons through whom His awesome power is aimed at those who need to be rescued from the Evil One.

Jesus gives us ample evidence of this latter kind of prayer. When He came down from the mountain after His transfiguration, he was shown a boy who was possessed of demons. In His absence, His disciples, had done their best in praying *to* God for the child to be delivered, but their efforts had been to no avail. When Jesus comes on the scene He refers to a special kind of prayer and fasting that builds up the spiritual dynamism which makes this kind of miracle possible (Mark 9:14–29). He then focuses the spiritual power that is within Him on the boy, and in a painful struggle with the demonic He victoriously delivers the boy to wholeness (Mark 9:25–27).

Jesus used prayer time as a time to be empowered by His Father. In fasting He had become conscious of the spirit and had been charged with a dynamism that could be directed against evil. Jesus surrendered Himself to all that His Father could impart to Him, and He came against the demons in the boy with their awesome spiritual energy.

In another situation Jesus is surrounded by a mob who are pressing in upon Him to receive blessings. In the crowd there was one particular woman who had been tortured with a condition that had her hemorrhaging constantly (Mark 5:24–34). It was probably vaginal bleeding, which in the Jewish culture meant that she was considered spiritually unclean and unfit to worship God.

When Jesus walked by, she reached out and touched Him. She was convinced that if she could just touch the hem of His garment, she would be healed. As she touched Jesus the hoped-for miracle occurred, and instantly Jesus felt power go out from Him (Mark 5:30). Jesus overcame the evil that caused this woman's suffering by allowing Himself to be a channel through whom His Father's healing power could flow.

We are supposed to be able to do what Jesus did. His demonstrations of power were demonstrations of a power that is available to all of us. What I am suggesting is that each of us should be open to an infilling of the power of God which can then be focused on a person or persons who need deliverance. Prayer and fasting can be a process whereby we, like Jesus, can become charged with the dynamism of God that then can be directed through us toward those persons who need to be rescued from the influence of dark powers.

A Case of Deliverance

The son of one of my friends was extremely caught up in the music of a rock group that made Satanism a part of its act. I am in no position to evaluate what was real or unreal about the evil dimensions of this rock group's concerts. What I do know is that my friend's son was deeply affected by the group and, over a year's time, had become a very different person. Whereas once he had a bright disposition and was interested in people, now he had gradually become depressed and increasingly detached. He developed an intense hostility toward his parents and a meanness toward his little brother. His very facial features seemed to change, and he took on an overt insolence when he talked to anyone who tried to relate to him.

At first his parents tried to tell themselves that what was happening was just a bad case of teenage rebellion and that their boy would soon pass through this stage and come out of it. But as time went on they started to have second thoughts and began to sense that something sinister was at work. There was evidence of drug use. The posters that he hung on the walls of his room were of evil fantasies. After much soul-searching they took him to a psychotherapist but received little help. The psychotherapist acknowledged that there was something wrong with the boy, but she could not put her finger on it, nor could she figure out what to do.

I met the boy one evening while visiting at his home. He came in while I was sitting at the dining-room table drinking coffee with his parents. His mother introduced me, and I said "Hi" in as friendly a fashion as I could. He never answered. He sneered, shook his head, and went upstairs to his bedroom. The total effect was shattering to the three of us that were left behind.

The following day I telephoned a Baptist pastor I knew whose church was just down the street from where this boy and his family lived. I told him that the boy needed help and I would be most appreciative if he could do something. This pastor knew the boy and also knew the group that he hung out with at night. He told me that this group was into things that were, in his words, "over their heads."

My pastor friend joined together with some of the young people in his church who were intensely committed Christians.

Each of them pledged themselves to a day of prayer and fasting. At the end of the day they got together, laid their hands on the pastor, and together they prayed for him to have power over demons. There was a sense that all of them had been filled by the Spirit, and they in turn were imparting what they had received to the pastor.

That evening the pastor went to visit the boy's home. He rang the doorbell, and the boy himself answered. The parents were not in. The pastor sat down with the boy and started the conversation with the simple words, "I've come to bring you to Jesus."

He did not have to say any more. The boy started to cry and tremble. My pastor friend went over and sat next to him and put his arm around him and claimed him in the name of Jesus.

The pastor then invited the boy to go back to the church with him and pray with the young people who were still there praying and waiting. For the next couple of hours they prayed and ministered to him.

When the boy went home that night he was a different person. His mother later told me that it was like an evil spell had been broken and her son had been rescued. I think she was right.

The pastor later explained to me that he and his young people believed that they had become channels through whom the Holy Spirit had been directed toward this boy. He said, in words reminiscent of what was once said by the Apostle Paul, "I came at him not with any prepared speech. I just came to him in the power of the Holy Spirit."

I am not sure little demons are lurking on shelves or hiding behind furniture waiting to get us. *As a matter of fact, there is some evidence in the Bible that demons cannot exist in such a disembodied form* (see Matt. 8:28–34). What I do know is that there are many people in our world who have fallen under the influence of evil and need to be delivered from the powers of darkness. To attack the evil in such persons is a form of spiritual warfare that requires a special kind of prayer and fasting.

Chapter 10

Getting Set for Battle

Spiritual warfare requires that we be properly equipped. This dangerous dimension of the Christian life requires prayerful preparation and a proper appraisal of our enemy. He will come at us in discussions at work and in university classrooms. He will try to seduce us through sexual enticements. Even in places where we might think that we are safe, like in the church, he goes to work to create disillusionment and despair. He will make us vulnerable to temptation by leading us into a state of burnout from Christian service. He will prod us into cynicism by drawing our attention to Christian leaders who have failed to live up to our expectations. He cleverly plans our destruction in a host of ways.

The Apostle Paul in Ephesians 6:13–18 employs an analogy to the armor worn by Roman soldiers going into battle as an outline of the ways that we should be equipped if we are to win out over our spiritual adversary. In a passage that has become a classic for those who talk of spiritual warfare he writes:

> Wherefore take unto you the whole armour of God, that ye may be able to withstand in the evil day, and having done all, to stand. Stand therefore, having your loins girt about

with truth, and having on the breastplate of righteousness; and your feet shod with the preparation of the gospel of peace; above all, taking the shield of faith, wherewith ye shall be able to quench all the fiery darts of the wicked. And take the helmet of salvation, and the sword of the Spirit, which is the word of God: praying always with all prayer and supplication in the Spirit, and watching thereunto with all perseverance and supplication for all saints.

The Belt of Truth

In spiritual warfare we begin with truth. Paul tells us in Ephesians 6:14 that truth should be our belt, that is, our most basic garment. From the beginning of time the demonic has used deception to ensnare God's people. Only those who have a confident knowledge of truth will survive. We must know what the Bible teaches and be firmly grounded in the basic creeds of the faith. We must know *what* we believe and *why* we believe it. As Peter instructs us:

> But sanctify the Lord God in your hearts: and be ready always to give an answer to every man that asketh you a reason of the hope that is in you with meekness and fear.
> *1 Peter 3:15*

In the Garden of Eden Satan was able to seduce both Adam and Eve by casting doubt on the word of God. The Evil One asks over and over again, "Are you absolutely sure about what God said?"

> Now the serpent was more subtle than any beast of the field which the Lord God had made. And he said unto the woman, Yea, hath God said, Ye shall not eat of every tree of the garden? And the woman said unto the serpent, We may eat of the fruit of the trees of the garden: but of the fruit of the tree

which is in the midst of the garden, God hath said, Ye shall not eat of it, neither shall ye touch it, lest ye die. And the serpent said unto the woman, Ye shall not surely die: for God doth know that in the day ye eat thereof, then your eyes shall be opened, and ye shall be as gods, knowing good and evil.

Genesis 3:1–5

Satan tries to give a deceitful "spin" to what the first couple "thinks" God said to them, and Adam and Eve are not sure enough of themselves to withstand the temptation. They buy the lie of Satan because they are not grounded in the truth. And the rest, as they say, is history.

Contrast the uncertainty about the truth so evident with the first Adam with the absolute confidence in scripture demonstrated by the Second Adam, Jesus, when Satan exercises his wiles against Him. In the temptation of Jesus recorded in Matthew 4, Satan tries the same tactic he employed on Adam and Eve in the garden. The Evil One tries to cast doubt on the meaning of the word of God. Quoting scripture in a way that twists its meaning, Satan endeavors to lead Jesus into sin. There is an attempt on Satan's part to provide theological justification for yielding to the attractive alternatives to the will of God. But the Second Adam is no easy prey for the attacks of the demonic. Jesus knows the Bible too well to fall for the tricks of Satan. Our Lord had studied the scriptures from His early youth. He *knew* the truth. He was sufficiently in touch with the biblical writings so as to provide quotes that corrected the distorted use of scriptures employed by His spiritual adversary. With truth, Jesus beat back the threats of the Evil One.

Recently I met up with an old friend from my teen years. He had attended the same church I did as a boy, and we had gone through high school together. Because of our past association I was more than a little disturbed when he let me know that he was deeply involved in the New Age movement. He had become a disciple of Shirley MacLaine and had swallowed all of that strange synthesis of the occult, Eastern mysticism, and the Human Potential movement that has become so widespread among many economically upscale, middle-class Yuppies. He went on and on about the sense of personal mastery and self-actualization he had discovered in his new philosophy and spiritual experiences.

I was very interested in why my friend had turned away from Christianity. I wanted to know how he came to reject the message of the Bible and to turn from the truth. "I haven't turned away from the Bible," he answered. "Actually I believe the Bible more today than I ever did. All the things I now believe were taught by Jesus. I just never realized it until I became enlightened by my new perspectives on the truth."

As my friend continued the description of his spiritual journey it became obvious that he had been enticed by what I believe to be a demonically inspired ideology because he did not have a firm and clear understanding of what the Bible teaches. Consequently, he hardly noticed when someone came along and linked New Age beliefs to some sayings of Jesus that were taken out of context and highly distorted. Instead, he was easily led into thinking that New Age philosophy was simply a natural extension of the teachings of Jesus. This would have never happened if he had been girded with the belt of truth.

In another case, a young woman who had grown up in a Christian home and had graduated from a Christian college became involved in an obscene cult called the Children of God. This heretical stepchild of the Jesus movement of the late 1960s is alleged to encourage its attractive female members to use sex as a means of luring men into their cult.

When I met this young woman on the streets of Milan, Italy, she was "witnessing" to whomever would listen to her. When I asked her how she could go to bed with a man in an effort to evangelize him, she responded, "After what Jesus did for me, there isn't anything I wouldn't do for Him."

I tried to explain to her that Jesus would never want her to do such things. But she simply told me that God's grace would cover everything and that the cost of winning a soul was never too much to pay.

As we talked together it was obvious that this unfortunate woman had very little understanding about what the Bible teaches and what the Lord expects of His people. She had been seduced by half-truths because she was unequipped with sound biblical teachings. She was easily corrupted by demonic forces because she had not been "girt about with truth."

Breastplate of Righteousness

According to Ephesians 6:14, the second piece of armor that the Christian must put on to carry out effective spiritual warfare is the "breastplate of righteousness." This may seem a bit strange when we discover that the breastplate of righteousness refers to the symbol of an Old Testament judge who goes among the people to ferret out and stop the injustices and oppression carried out against the downtrodden and the poor (Isa. 59:16–17).

Paul appears to be suggesting that if we are to defeat demonic spirits, we must destroy the environment of social evil in which they thrive. In situations fraught with injustice Satan is able to stir up hatred, resentment, and bitterness among the oppressed (Eph. 4:30–31). He is also able to encourage sadistic authoritarianism and prideful delusions of grandeur among the oppressors. These social-psychological conditions generated in the consciousness of people who live out their lives where justice is ignored and where exploitation is common proves to be fertile soil for demonic possession.

I believe the resentments nurtured in Adolf Hitler by the humiliation and economic oppression of the German people following World War I, the result of the terms of the Treaty of Versailles, made him vulnerable to demonic possession. The same can be said of Iraq's Saddam Hussein. What this Arab leader experienced as an impoverished youth under British occupation made him wildly hostile. What his people endured as Western nations allowed the unjust humiliation of Palestinians generated an insatiable hunger for revenge. Once again, I believe injustices and oppression created a person who was open to recruitment into the legions of the Evil One.

Paul calls upon us to carry on spiritual warfare by eliminating conditions in which demons can fester. He asks us to put on a breastplate of righteousness and, like the judges of the Old Testament, to wipe out the conditions that make people easy targets for evil spirits. The defeat of Satan and his hosts is contingent on creating justice and ending oppression. To this end Jesus leads the charge against the demonic legions. The Bible says of Him:

> Behold my servant, whom I have chosen; my beloved, in whom my soul is well pleased: I will put my spirit upon him, and he shall show judgment to the Gentiles. He shall not strive, nor cry; neither shall any man hear his voice in the streets. A bruised reed shall he not break, and smoking flax shall he not quench, till he send forth judgment unto victory. And in his name shall the Gentiles trust.
>
> *Matthew 12:18–20*

Charles Finney, the evangelist whom many historians label the Billy Graham of the nineteenth century, understood this truth with great clarity. In his famous lectures on the "Conditions for Revival," Finney goes to great length to link spiritual warfare with crusades for social justice. He said that if Satan was to be defeated, then the social conditions that made people open to demonic possession must be eliminated.

In the 1830s, when Finney did most of his preaching, this meant that slavery had to be abolished and the equality of women had to be established. He believed that what was happening to blacks and to women was breeding attitudes and dispositions that made people prime subjects for the powers of darkness. Both the Abolitionist movement and the modern Feminist movement can trace their roots to this revivalist who linked social justice with spiritual warfare.

The Footwear of the Saints

In Ephesians 6:15, Paul next directs us to prepare for battles against evil by having our "feet shod with the preparation of the gospel of peace." Quite simply, this means that our feet should be set in the starting blocks so that we are ready to run anywhere we must and go to anyone who needs us to do the work of reconciliation. How many churches are spiritually weak and vulnerable to demonic havoc because their members are divided and arguing with each other? How many families are spiritually dry and open to demonic influences because members are allowing misunderstandings and differing attitudes to set them in opposition to each other? How many people have provided opportunities for dark powers to be harbored within them because they maintain an unforgiving spirit toward those whom they believe have hurt them?

If we are to be able to withstand the onslaught of the Evil One, then we must be ready to rush about to be reconciled to people and to carry on a ministry of reconciliation between those who are alienated from each other. "And all things are of God, who hath reconciled us to himself by Jesus Christ, and hath given to us the ministry of reconciliation" (2 Cor. 5:18).

In the New Testament we find a brilliant example of reconciliation and peace in Barnabas. It is Barnabas who brings the converted Paul into reconciliation with the church that he had once persecuted. It is easy to understand the hesitancy of those first-century Christians when Paul sought their acceptance. Paul was the man who had made life hell for them and in many ways was considered their most serious enemy. But Barnabas was intent on bringing Paul and the church together. He was a man of reconciliation. His feet were "shod with the preparation of the gospel of peace."

Satan might have won a great victory if Barnabas had not been prepared to make peace between Paul and the rest of the Christian community. The church would have been weak without its greatest theologian and its people less equipped to carry out spiritual warfare without his insightful writings. Without Paul the spiritual dynamism of the church would have been diminished, and the army of God would have been less viable in its battles against the powers of darkness.

In another instance Barnabas was the peacemaker between Paul and the young John Mark. During the first missionary journey John Mark had reneged on his commitment to travel with Paul and Barnabas and, in the face of persecution, abandoned them to return to Antioch. Later, when John Mark had repented and asked to be given another chance to serve as a missionary, Paul remained hostile. It was Barnabas who made peace between these two men and in so doing saved John Mark for a life of future ministry. We would not have the Book of Mark in the New Testament if Barnabas had not rescued him from despair by being an instrument of peace.

In our own time we have a brilliant example of a man whose feet were "shod with the preparation of the gospel of peace" in President Jimmy Carter. Satan had wrought his destruction through numerous wars between the Egyptians and the Israelis. The demons had free reign in the lives of the millions of people who had been set against each other in hateful conflict. Then this Baptist Sunday school teacher and world leader, Jimmy Carter, stepped between Anwar Sadat and Menachem Begin and made peace.

Carter brought Sadat and Begin together at Camp David. Housing them in separate bungalows, he served as an errand boy between the two of them, negotiating a settlement to the conflict between these two leaders and their nations. Eventually Carter was able to bring the two of them together and build a peace between their nations. And Satan suffered another major defeat.

Spiritual warfare requires that we be peacemakers. To defeat the designs of the Evil One each of us must be ready to pray the prayer of Francis of Assisi:

> Lord, make me an instrument of thy peace.
> Where there is hatred, let me sow love;
> Where there is injury, pardon;
> Where there is doubt, faith;
> Where there is despair, hope;
> Where there is darkness, light;
> Where there is sadness, joy.
> O Divine Master, grant that I may not so much seek
> To be consoled as to console,
> To be understood as to understand,
> To be loved as to love.
> For it is in giving that we receive,
> It is in pardoning that we are pardoned,
> And it is in dying that we are born to eternal life.

Taking the Shield of Faith

Above all, we are told in Ephesians 6:16, we must take up the shield of faith wherewith we will be able to quench all the fiery darts of the wicked one. This faith is a gift of the Holy Spirit that is given to those who pray for it. It is this faith that gives us the confidence to endure whatever Satan throws at us. Faith, in the end, is what keeps us from going under spiritually when we are beset by discouragements and disappointments. It is faith that, above all else, is our best defense against the attacks of the demonic armies.

Sometimes I find that Christian service is more than I can handle. So many things go wrong. So many efforts end in failure. So many good intentions result in problems. Sometimes I feel like no good deed goes unpunished, and I want to give up. Fortunately I have an assistant who knows how to rekindle my faith through prayer. She often makes me stop everything and join her before the Lord. She helps to renew my faith and to regain confidence. She helps me to see that the defeats are only temporary and the discouragements are only passing. She helps me to reaffirm that I may experience losses and setbacks, but they are all in a cause that will eventually triumph. And she reminds me that it is better to lose in a cause that ultimately wins than to win in a cause that will ultimately lose.

I get a bit ticked off at those who make it a habit of picking on my friends Robert Schuller and Norman Vincent Peale. The critics of these preachers of positive thinking and possibility thinking fail to see that what these men say to people is grounded in their faith in Jesus Christ. These two prominent Christian leaders live in the confidence that if God be for us then no evil forces can ultimately prevail against us. They want us to live in the certainty that evil will not triumph in our lives if we put our confidence in God. Their optimism is no blind Pollyanna disposition to life. Instead it is grounded in the assurance that greater is He that is in me than he who is in the world (1 John 4:4). To know in the depths of our being that the Holy Spirit will empower us sufficiently to assure victory in all of life's circumstances is at the core of the gospel that they preach. They are intent upon getting us to see that Jesus has demonstrated in the resurrection that all the powers of darkness together could not keep Him down and that this same triumphant power can be alive in us through the Holy Spirit.

You may think that the Crystal Cathedral is a waste of money and that positive thinking does not take sin seriously enough, but do not fail to see that Schuller and Peale have become heralds of hope in a world all too filled with pessimism. Henry Ford once said, "If you think you can or you think you can't, either way you are right." Henry Ford knew that confidence is the basis for all victories, and to that we as Christians will have to say Amen!

Our confidence is great because it is not in ourselves but in Christ. We know that we cannot be defeated by demonic powers because we have the same Spirit in us that triumphed over all the evil in the cosmos when Christ was raised from the dead (Rom. 8:11).

If we ever lack the kind of faith we need we only have to pray that it be given. The Holy Spirit provides such faith for those who ask for it. The Spirit gives us "the shield of faith, wherewith ye shall be able to quench all the fiery darts of the wicked." He gives us deliverance from the doubts and discouragements that make us vulnerable to what the powers of darkness would do to us: "Thanks be to God, which giveth us the victory through our Lord Jesus Christ!" (1 Cor. 15:57–58).

The Helmet of Salvation

Often we fail to recognize that salvation is an ongoing process in our lives. When Paul tells us in Ephesians 6:17 to put on the helmet of salvation, he is really telling us to put ourselves under the continual transforming work of God. Salvation is much more than what God did for us in Jesus on the cross. It is also work that the Holy Spirit does in us and through us day by day and moment by moment. We *were* saved when we trusted in what Jesus achieved for us; we are *being* saved daily through the ongoing ministry of the Holy Spirit; and we *will be* saved when we are perfected in the presence of God on that final day (1 John 3:2).

In spiritual warfare those who put on the helmet of salvation are people who have subjected themselves to the continuing regenerating power of God that enables us to win victories. The struggle against Satan and his demonic army would exhaust us. The energy used up in maintaining vigilance against temptations and in warding off the negative influences constantly being aimed at us would leave us spiritually debilitated. But the good news is that we can be connected to the renewing power of God. Through the Holy Spirit, He can recharge us so that we have the vitality to carry on the struggle against evil. If we remain connected to Him "with all prayer and supplication in the Spirit," there is a saving power that will deliver us from the tendencies toward personal entropy. Through the renewing of our minds and hearts, we are no longer easy victims for the evil one.

I find myself fascinated by solar engines. These modern contraptions seem to be able to function with consistent efficiency so long as their solar panels are turned toward the sun. The source of energy is constant and, insofar as its panels are positioned to collect that energy as it radiates toward earth, the engine runs with optimum effectiveness.

Those who wear the helmet of salvation are those who position themselves to receive the constant flow of spiritual energy that comes to us from God. They are people who are plugged into the source of power that enables us to be more than conquerors over those dark forces that would defeat us.

Most of us can recall times of great spiritual energy wherein we felt confident that we could live out the Christian life victoriously. We attended revival meetings, Bible conferences, and spiritual retreats that infused us with a dynamic that made us sure that Satan could have no quarter with us. Unfortunately, we often fail to recognize that this energy dissipates quickly, and we are left without the strength to endure temptations. An ongoing renewal of the saving power of God is essential if we are to be strong enough for spiritual warfare. Being connected to that power and having it surge through us comes from being constantly aware of and surrendered to the ongoing work of God. That is what Paul means when he talks about wearing the helmet of salvation.

To enjoy the ongoing work of salvation in your life, it is essential that you become a part of the church. The church is the body of Christ, and those who are willing to be fitted into His body experience a continual ministry of His healing and sustaining presence.

There are so many people who wrongly think that salvation is only a matter of trusting in Jesus for the forgiveness of sins. They do not understand that to be saved is to be part of a saving community of fellow Christians who will pray for them, hold them accountable for their lifestyles, and provide them with the teachings that will encourage and build them up in Christ.

Be careful that the particular congregation of the church that you join is alive in Christ, has a nurturing fellowship, and has a deep sense of responsibility toward each of its members. Look for a community of believers that will enable you to feel loved and looked after. Make sure that the church you join is made up of real people who can be honest with one another and who are not ashamed to confess their sins one to another. Be certain that it has a membership that is deeply involved in a collective prayer life and that its people know how to worship in dynamic ways that create an awareness of the Holy Spirit.

I know that what I am calling for is a tall order. But if the ongoing work of salvation is to be realized and enjoyed, than being connected to a church that is alive in the Holy Spirit is essential.

Some churches are dead. You can feel the deadness when you walk into their morning worship services. Do not waste your time on dead churches. You need to wear the helmet of salvation, and only a vital church can offer one to you.

I believe that a good measure of a church can be had in the context of sharing Holy Communion. When the congregation takes the bread and the wine, there should be a sense of the real presence of Jesus. In the remembrance of His broken body and shed blood there should be an awareness of something mystically glorious going on. When I am in such a setting I want to experience the God who continues to save me and make me His own. I want to become a participant in a body that sustains the vitality that is essential for spiritual warfare. In Holy Communion I can sense if a particular church is a church that can help me.

163

Taking Up the Sword of the Spirit

The final piece of equipment to be taken up by the Christian in spiritual warfare is the "sword of the Spirit, which is the word of God" (Eph. 6:17). It is the ultimate weapon to be used in beating back the Evil One. Satan cannot bear to hear the word of God being declared.

It may seem hard to imagine that the simple forthtelling of the gospel and the declaration of God's judgment upon the princes of darkness could be so powerful. Yet it is through "the foolishness of preaching" that the heaviest damage is done to those who would attack God's people (1 Cor. 1:21).

In Genesis, when God speaks, the darkness is split in two and the universe is brought into being. It is by the word of Yahweh that the heavens are formed and the creatures of the land and sea are created. When, in the New Testament, Jesus speaks, the powers of death are overcome and corpses are resurrected (John 10:1–42). The word of our Lord drives out demons (Mark 9:25) and stills troubled waters (Mark 4:39). His word, says the scriptures, will not return unto Him void, but it will accomplish that which it is intended to do (Isa. 55:11).

The miraculous powers of the word of God are not confined to the utterances of Jesus. There are times when we ourselves speak and discover that His powerful words are put in our mouths (Matt. 10:19). Not every religious statement, sermon, or prophesy that we utter has this kind of power, but when the Holy Spirit infuses our words it happens. The Spirit of God can overshadow us and impart to what we say an awesome dynamism that drives back the encroaching presence of evil.

I was the guest for a chapel service at a Christian college that was known for its strong commitment to the Charismatic movement. The reputation of this school's spirituality was such that I was a bit intimidated being there. I had the sense that I would be exposed as being an inferior Christian before the day

164

was over. Everyone I met at the college spoke in that super-religious vocabulary that is constantly punctuated by what I call Pentecostal jargon. There were constant references to what the Lord was doing in the school and in their lives. They all talked about how close to God they felt and what the Lord was doing in their lives.

In spite of all the lofty talk and references to the work of the Spirit, I had a strange and overwhelming sense that people in this school were playing the game of the emperor's new clothes. As in the story by Hans Christian Andersen, everyone seemed to be pretending to experience what really was not real. I sensed that out of a fear of being deemed blind to spiritual realities if the truth were admitted, people allowed themselves to live out a lie.

As I took to the pulpit for the chapel service, I prayed intensely that the Holy Spirit would give me the words that I should say. I prayed that I would be free from the oppressive and depressing feeling that had me weighed down.

When I started to speak I found myself preaching something other than my prepared message. I almost could not believe what I was hearing from my own mouth. My first words were, "There is a great deal of phoniness around here. There is a lot of pretending going on. I believe that Satan has nurtured a spirit of dishonesty among us so that we are afraid to be open and forthright about our spiritual condition. We are a people who are enslaved to a lie. We are pretending to have a real and satisfying infilling of the Spirit. The truth is that there is a dryness in our hearts, and behind our plastic smiles there is a depression that we are reluctant to reveal."

I was shocked at my daring declaration. And yet, even as I spoke I realized that my words were doing things to people. They cut through a veneer of superficial religiosity and laid bare a spiritual wasteland. In an instant the demonic hold that had held sway over that audience was broken. There was release which was quickly followed by an outpouring of the Spirit. As the scripture says,

> For the word of God is quick, and powerful, and sharper than
> any twoedged sword, piercing even to the dividing asunder
> of soul and spirit, and of the joints and marrow, and is a dis-
> cerner of the thoughts and intents of the heart.
>
> *Hebrews 4:12*

When the chapel time was over nobody left. We stayed together confessing and praying. The Spirit of God flowed with
awesome power among us. Yes, some people prayed in tongues,
but there was no recrimination toward those who did not. There
was an awareness that the measure of spirituality among us had
more to do with how honest we were being with each other than
with the exercising of any spiritual gifts. I knew that I had spoken
a word from God and it had proved to be the sword of the spirit
that breaks the chains of spiritual bondage and wards off the attacks of the Wicked One.

The kind of thing that happened in that college chapel can
happen on the personal level in our relationships with one another. M. Scott Peck in his book *People of the Lie* contends that the
demonic possession he has encountered in his work as a psychotherapist has always been with very religious people who lied to
others and eventually to themselves about who and what they
were. Honesty is a prerequisite to spirituality, but unfortunately
religious people have a great propensity for being fakes.

There is no hope for the infilling of the Spirit if we pretend
that we are already Spirit-filled. God can give us nothing if we
deceptively act as if we already have the gift. Jesus said that pros-
titutes and sinners who are honest about their condition are more
likely to enter the kingdom of God than are those who, like the
Pharisees in his day, pretend to already be spiritually complete
(Matt. 21:23–31).

It is a Christian responsibility to be courageous enough to
speak the truth in the face of religious deceptions. When persons
are not being real, we must not allow them to continue their

charades. If we speak the word of God in such situations, we must do so in love and prayer.

We must go on more than a hunch. We must lean on the Lord and ask Him to direct us in what we say. Actually, discerning the spirits is a spiritual gift from God (1 Cor. 12:10), and we should pray that God would give us this gift before we speak. But speaking the word of God in the face of phoniness and calling people to honesty is essential if we are to fight off Satan and counteract what he can do to us when we play out our games of hypocrisy.

Chapter 11

Wrapping It Up

There are three expressions of the Holy Spirit in the Book of Acts. There's the wind, which symbolizes the new life that the Spirit brings. There is the fire, which denotes the purifying work that the Spirit carries out in our lives. And there are the tongues, which symbolize the communication that makes estranged people one.

> And when the day of Pentecost was fully come, they were all with one accord in one place. And suddenly there came a sound from heaven as of a rushing mighty wind, and it filled all the house where they were sitting. And there appeared unto them cloven tongues like as of fire, and it sat upon each of them. And they were all filled with the Holy Ghost, and began to speak with other tongues, as the Spirit gave them utterance.
>
> *Acts 2:1–4*

If there is any theme that should be highlighted in our discussions of the Holy Spirit it is the theme of the new life that Christians experience when the Spirit fills them and vibrates through their being. Everywhere I go I encounter Christians who believe all the right things and even trust in the work of Christ on the cross as the basis for their salvation, but they lack the kind of vital aliveness that can come through total surrender to the ministry of the Holy Spirit. They are people who have all the forms of godliness but seem lacking in that spiritual dynamism that should mark the Christian off from the world.

John Wesley was certainly conscious of being in such a condition even as he served as a missionary to Georgia. He knew that he lacked subjective assurance that he belonged to God, and he was more than conscious that he was devoid of the joyfulness that is supposed to belong to those who are in Christ. But one evening at a prayer meeting in a small building on Aldersgate Street in London, the Spirit came upon him. From then on Wesley knew of the new life that the Holy Spirit can generate in the Christian and how the Spirit can take the deadness of the soul away. The Holy Spirit came upon Wesley like a wind, and he experienced being a Christian in a whole new way.

What happened to Wesley can happen to all of us if we are but willing to be surrendered to what the Spirit wills to effect in our lives.

Second, there is the purifying work of the Spirit that delivers us from the effects of sin. So many of us need this fire in our lives. There are countless Christians who believe that their sins are forgiven and that God has forgotten their sins, but they are still burdened with the haunting memory of what they have done. They need a purging of these memories. They need to have the things of the past burned away.

There are others who live in the fantasies of sin. They are people who on the surface seem decent and upright but who allow their minds to indulge in sexual relationships that are fraught with evil. There is the man who maintains a faithful relationship with his wife but then resorts to pornography for some private thrills. He tells himself that he is not hurting anybody, but all the time he is slowly becoming jaded so that his normal relations with his wife come to be dull and devoid of gratification. There is the woman who is constantly fantasizing about the possible excitement and fulfillment that would be hers if she could just be in the arms of a particular man. She knows that being in that relationship would be sinful, so she does not make any moves to negotiate the relationship, but she allows her every idle moment to be consumed with her fantasy. These are only a couple of cases of the countless Christians who need to be purified. They need the Spirit who comes like a cleansing fire upon any who will ask for His Baptism.

Perhaps you are one of those who is keenly aware of a need for being purified. Maybe you have been longing for the cleansing of heart and mind that can deliver you from the effects of an ugly consciousness. The good news is that the Holy Spirit wills to make you pure in heart if you only plead for this to happen.

Lastly, Christians long for intimacy, which is what real communication is all about. The image of *koinonia* is incredibly enticing. The need for unconditional love and caring is a basic hunger. We all want relationships in which there are no barriers to honest communication. We all crave the sense of oneness that comes when we feel we are with people who completely and empathetically understand us.

When the Day of Pentecost came upon the church, that is what happened. People who came from different ethnic backgrounds and represented different perspectives on life suddenly discovered a oneness in the Holy Spirit that met their deepest needs for fellowship. The Holy Spirit created oneness and perfect communication, all of which was symbolized by tongues coming upon them.

A group of my students from Eastern College went to Haiti for a short-term missionary experience. When they returned, there was a noticeable change in the demeanor of several of them. When I inquired about the trip, two students explained that they had met God in Haiti. This response surprised me, because I knew these students were Christians before they went on the trip. But the students explained that they had only *believed* the gospel before going to Haiti. They claimed that it wasn't until they had worshiped with Haitian Christians that they had really *met* God.

As they had shared in a Sunday morning worship service, these students had become open to the Holy Spirit and He had performed the miracle of tongues. Students who could not understand a word of the Creole language gained a miraculous sense of oneness with Haitian brothers and sisters. At the deepest levels of their being they encountered an understanding with people who were very culturally different. Their knowledge of them was deeper than cognitive knowledge. It was more profound than the kind of sharing that goes with ordinary verbal discourse. It was an understanding shared by those who are one in the Spirit of God.

All of us need that kind of miracle. There are husbands and wives who talk *at* each other but don't communicate on the ultimately important levels of life. There are mothers who can't communicate with their daughters, fathers who can't communicate with their sons. They talk to each other, but they never seem to make contact. They are people who need the miracle of the Spirit.

In the workplace and in the church there are situations that also cry out for real communication. Words fly. Sermons are preached. Statements are made. But little understanding occurs. There is a desperate need for the miracle of the Spirit. The need for a special work of the Spirit is all too obvious.

How Much Do You Want It?

The question that begs for an answer is whether you desperately *want* a special infilling of the Holy Spirit at this time in your life. What I have been discussing in this little book is not some extra frill to the Christian life or some kind of added nutrient that will give you a bit more zest to living out the Christian life. The Holy Spirit is for those who "hunger and thirst." The infilling is for those who are conscious of a dryness of soul that is intolerable. It is for those who need a power that might rescue a loved one who is slipping toward the darkness and seems indifferent to the pleadings and arguments of others. The baptism of the Spirit is for people who are aware that there is something much deeper to the Christian life than what they are experiencing.

Furthermore, you should be well aware that such an infilling comes at a very high price. You must be ready to yield up your life to whatever God wants to do in you and through you. You must be so intense in your desire to know Him and the power that was revealed in His resurrection that you are willing to let yourself die to everything that you have been about in life.

That I may know him, and the power of his resurrection, and the fellowship of his sufferings, being made conformable unto his death.

Philippians 3:10

Everything from sexual cravings to ego-gratifying pride must be put on the block. You must be ready to have everything about yourself changed, even the basic motivations of your life.

The Spirit comes to those who are ready for total surrender. Do you want this infilling enough to take such a step?

When Siddhartha was still a boy, he traveled to a mountain retreat in search of a certain sage who supposedly knew the answers to all the secrets of life. Siddhartha wanted to find God, and he believed that this sage could help him.

After much effort Siddhartha found the sage and made his inquiry. The man and the boy talked for a while. Then the sage bade Siddhartha to follow him. He took the boy to the edge of a lake and there they sat and talked some more.

Suddenly the sage grabbed the young Siddhartha by the throat, plunged his head beneath the water, and held him there.

Siddhartha tried to escape from the iron grip, but the sage was far too strong for him. Siddhartha was sure that he would die.

Just as the young Siddhartha was about to give up and accept the fate of death, the sage suddenly pulled him out of the water.

Siddhartha gasped for air. It took him several minutes to regain his breath. And at that moment, when Siddhartha was about to cry out in protest, the sage raised his hand and silenced him.

Then the sage said to Siddhartha, "When you want God as desperately as you have just wanted breath, then, and only then, will you find Him."

Christians must learn from this story. If we are to experience the real presence of God, then we must have this kind of desperate earnestness. In the words of scripture, we must seek Him with all of our heart, mind, soul, and strength.

If you really crave the Spirit and seek the infilling with all your heart, it will happen. It may not come instantaneously, and it may only come after painful struggles within your heart and mind. But the scripture promises:

> Ask, and it shall be given you; seek, and ye shall find; knock, and it shall be opened unto you . . .
> *Matthew 7:7*

And the scriptures do not lie!